faith moves

LEAVING COMFORT
FOR YOUR CALLING

faith moves

LEAVING COMFORT FOR YOUR CALLING

W. Seth Martin

ISBN: 9798832784007

Edited by Tiffani Bowe
Layout and formatting by Graphics.tif
Book cover design by Muse Media
Photography by Drew Bryant

Printed in the United States of America
Printed by Kindle Direct Publishing, An Amazon.com Company
Copyright © 2022 William Seth Martin
All rights reserved.

Patience,

I pray this work encourages

you.

To my wife, Hannah:

*The love of my life who has trusted me to
hear from God and lead our family.
Thank you for being my partner in life.
The faith moves we've made have been sweet
because we have each other.*

To my parents, Ken and Laura Martin:

Thank you for modeling active faith in me and my siblings' lives.

Contents

FOREWORD

Do we truly TRUST God? What does it mean to sincerely operate in faith? Does our faith require us to make moves that from the outside may seem foolish and outlandish? How do we move past making *"Trust in the Lord with all your heart, and lean not onto your own understanding"* more than an easily quoted bible verse? How do we begin to actively pursue God's plans for our lives even when we don't fully understand the plans ourselves? How do we move forward when family and friends aren't on board, don't see the vision, or perhaps challenge the purpose God placed on our heart? How do we leave behind the comfort and familiarity of what we are used to for the promise of the unknown? These questions and others are explored with authenticity in *Faith Moves,* a book by my brother and friend, Pastor Seth Martin, lead servant and teacher of the Brook Community Church in Minneapolis, Minnesota.

With close to 20 years of pastoral experience, on more than one occasion, I have found myself wrestling with the "safe" choice versus the vision God placed on my heart. Two years ago, COVID changed the world as we knew it. The Church and our perception of faith was not exempt from this. I could argue religious organizations were possibly one of the hardest hit entities. The inability to worship together exacerbated the toll this disease took on our mental and emotional health.

The fear of the unknown, the daunting reality that things may never be the same, and the desire to not "rock the boat" and just make it to the other side of this pandemic caused complacency during this season. Many times, It seemed like the smartest decision was to do nothing, play it safe, and just ride out the season. However, despite the challenges that this pandemic has imposed, I still saw the vision of "one church in multiple locations" be developed and enhanced with TabGLOBAL, *Tabernacle Baptist Church*'s interactive digital campus. Our church also broke ground and moved forward with plans for our third campus. When God gives you a dream, he knows what it will cost, the mistakes you will make, and the lessons you will learn. God has already did the math and worked through the calculations. Therefore, if you commit to the dream and vision, God will handle the rest. It is true, for every God "vision" there is God "provision."

Pastor Seth provides a reflective, witty, real world applicative work of how to recognize the challenges that are blocking us from fulfilling God's call on our lives, while also providing encouragement and examples of the power of true proactive faith. Pastor Seth has served well at a multicultural and multiethnic church in the heart of Minneapolis, a city that has been at the center of social justice and racial inequality in the U.S. since the murder of George Floyd in 2020. With that as a backdrop, as well as starting a church in a new city, Pastor Seth knows what it means to dream big, step out, and make faith moves.

Faith Moves serves as a dynamic reminder that we serve one God, and his promises are sovereign over any plans we could make for ourselves. The key to recognizing our destiny lies in moving past the familiar and not tiptoeing, but rather, marching out on faith while trusting God on the unpredictable but certain journey.

As you read *Faith Moves*, it is my prayer that you recognize, as I did, what is holding you back from fully blossoming in your God-ordained destiny. I pray that this book can help you to discern God's voice and vision from Satan's seeds of uncertainty and fear. I pray that you will break free from the shackles of comfort to wholeheartedly and intentionally pursue your true divine purpose. I pray that this book serves as a useful tool in your spiritual tool belt, reminding you that faith is an action word. Experiencing the life that God truly desires for you is dependent upon putting sincere action behind your belief; an abiding belief that God will do what God said he would do.

Whatever your reason for picking up this book, my prayer is that this journey will make you better, brighter, bolder, and more willing to move forward in faith.

I remain a "FAITH MOVER,"

Dr. Charles E. Goodman, Jr.
Senior Pastor/Teacher
Tabernacle Baptist Church

PREFACE

"Say his name…GEORGE FLOYD!"

"Say his name…GEORGE FLOYD!"

I heard these words ringing through the air, day and night, as I sat on the couch in the living room of my home in Minneapolis. I lived only two blocks from where this black man was murdered by a white police officer. The murder set the world ablaze. In numerous cities, protesters filled the streets. Police fitted themselves with riot gear as military trucks patrolled the area. Tear gas filled the air, and buildings burned. The riots were the result of people who had grown weary of racism.

Corrupt law enforcement policies in the United States led to worldwide protests. Floyd's murder was the match that ignited a movement, and here I was right in the middle of it. You see, the church I planted and pastored happened to be in the same neighborhood where the crime took place. Some may suggest it was just by chance that I was so close to the catalytic event that caused so much social unrest. But as a person of faith, I don't believe it was a coincidence that this horrific crime occurred in the same neighborhood where I lived. I see it as providence, something divinely orchestrated and positioned by God. At the right time, God pushed me into a much greater purpose that would bring him glory. This positioning for purpose started years before the murder of George Floyd. It started when I made a *faith move*, a practical decision with real consequences without earthly assurances.

My wife and I demonstrated a faith move when we relocated from Chicago, Illinois, to Minneapolis, Minnesota, to establish and cultivate a church. We didn't have money, job security, a meeting location, or even a home. All we had was a leading by God to go to a new place and assurance from him that there he would use us for his glory. That one faith move positioned my wife and me to be in the middle of a worldwide movement. Most importantly, for a brief moment, it put God's message at the center of it all.

God didn't just position me to be in close proximity to the site of the murder. He also positioned me to assist with the community's response in its aftermath. Our church, which is multi-ethnic, organized peaceful protests. We leveraged my relationships with other pastors to push churches who wouldn't have normally participated in such events to get involved. Somehow that landed me on several media outlets including CNN, The Washington Post, and FOX News affiliates. I even spoke virtually in Australia. On every one of those outlets, my message was the same: Jesus cares about justice, and he can heal the human condition that leads to injustice. The church leveraged the platform that the chaos created to tell the world that Jesus cares and can heal the pain. I was given the opportunity to spread a message of hope to the world. But being where I needed to be to share that message all traced back to our original faith move.

INTRODUCTION

> **"...Without faith it is impossible to please him,
> for whoever would draw near to God
> must believe that he exists and that he
> rewards those who seek him."**

Hebrews 11:6 ESV

 ## Faith Explained

To understand the concept of faith, one must first learn the character of God. The God of Scripture exists eternally outside of time. The God who spoke and out of nothing came everything. The God who positioned every tree in its place sent the wind to make its leaves blow. The God who spoke and calmed raging oceans. The God who created mankind in his image blew life into our bodies and remains involved in the intricate details of our lives. When mankind ran away from him, God took on the form of humanity to bring us back, and guide those who believe in him. The God revealed to Moses as I AM. The one King David referred to as a Shepherd, and the one Jesus calls Father.

As Scripture describes it, faith is inextricably intertwined with God because it depends on him, who is perfectly faithful. It is the belief that God will keep his promises because he is faithful. Perhaps, it is best summed up by the word *trust*. This concept is a common thread in the Bible. In a passage of Scripture about vision and purpose, God says "the righteous shall live by faith" (Habakkuk 2:4 ESV).

Simply put, God is pleased with those who live their lives by faith (trust) in him. The Bible doubles down on this in several places and conveys faith is the only way to please God. Hebrews 11 maps out some of the most prominent believers in the pages of Scripture and reveals a common thread: they all had faith. Here are some examples: *by faith* Abraham ("The Patriarch of Israel") obeyed God and left his home to go to another land, *by faith* the people of Israel crossed the Red Sea on dry land, and *by faith* Rahab (a prostitute) was saved from death by giving men of God a place to hide, though it could've gotten her killed. Every example points to one truth, namely, that God is most pleased with our lives when we trust in Him.

 ## Faith has Feet

When I talk about *faith,* I'm not just talking about a belief in God for something. I'm not just talking about intrinsic belief. I'm not even talking about belief in Jesus for salvation, though that is the apex of faith. I'm talking about faith in God exposed through a human activity that changes the world. I'm talking about how faith *moves*. Faith has feet. Faith isn't just about believing; it's about doing something based on what you believe. Faith isn't stagnant or passive. Faith is active. Demonstrating genuine faith requires us to make firm decisions that wholeheartedly put our trust in God.

 ## Chess Moves

Faith moves are a lot like chess moves. In the game of chess, you don't make decisions based on your current position. You make them based on what's coming next. So it goes for faith moves in life. They are preemptive. They may not make sense now, but they make sense for what

God's going to do next. *Faith moves* position you to know and walk in your purpose. They lead you to the platforms that God destined just for you. *Purpose* is the fulfillment of what God has placed you on the earth to do and who he has called you to be. Apart from knowing God, knowing and living out your purpose is every person's greatest desire.

With earnest conviction, I believe that God has placed a divine calling and purpose on every single one of us (Ephesians 2:10). In case no one has ever told you, let me be the first to tell you that your life is not an accident or happenstance. It is an intentional, purposeful, direct result of God's providence and plans. God has designed you to be and to do something significant. The measure of our success in life is not determined by how much money we make, the status we attain, or the possessions we acquire. Rather, it is determined by how well we live out our calling and live up to our potential. Many people know this intuitively or discover it at some point in their life. So, if people know they have a purpose beyond simply working and paying bills, why don't they live their purpose? That question has prompted me to write this book. I believe some people get stuck. Some people miss getting positioned for purpose because they play it safe. They get caught in the subtle traps of life that dampen their purpose, causing them to live in fear and not in faith. This is not uncommon, nor is it something to be ashamed of. I'd venture to say it happens to everyone at some point in their lives. But that's why I wrote this book. I don't want you to live in fear. I want to help you get unstuck. I want you to be set free from the traps and make faith moves because one move today may put you in the middle of a movement tomorrow. I hope this book encourages you to leave places of familiarity and fear and make moves of faith. While familiarity entices you to live in fear, destiny demands you to live by faith.

 ## The Enemy of Destiny

One of the greatest enemies to our destiny is familiarity, and addressing this challenge is this book's purpose. Familiarity is a trap that inhibits us from making faith moves, effectively preventing us from shaping the world around us and reaching our God-given potential. Clinging to familiar surroundings confines us to live beneath our potential and frustrates our God-given purpose. Therefore, we must avoid the trap of familiarity to reach our God-given destiny. This trap is not a trap that randomly exists. Familiarity is a trap that Satan, the enemy against your destiny, intentionally sets. He understands that sowing seeds of fear in our hearts about the unfamiliar is the key to undermining our potential. That's his goal; to get you to live beneath the places God has called you to soar above. But remember, in situations that the enemy wants us to face in fear, God wants us to confront it with faith. God's best exists beyond our comfort zone.

When we cling to familiar, safe, and comfortable surroundings, we miss what God has for us.

After reading this book, I hope that you will make bold choices to move away from familiar spaces. God will lead you to new places emotionally, mentally, physically, and even geographically where you can reach your full potential and have a positive influence on the world. If only you will allow him. I hope after you've read this book—or maybe even while you read it—you'll make faith moves the way God destined you to!

CHAPTER *1*
The Truth About Traps ⟵

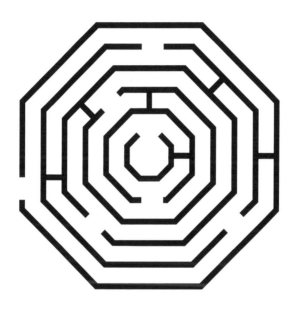

"The heart is more deceitful above
all things, and desperately sick;
who can understand it."

Jeremiah 17:9 ESV

The Nature of Traps:

You know what makes a good liar? A good liar's lies are made up of nine parts truth and only one part lie. Like a chemist carefully conducting an experiment or a chef masterfully crafting a dish, they get the measurements just right. The lies they tell are accurate enough to make you believe them but deceptive enough to…well, to deceive you. In their nature, traps are the same way. They offer more of what looks appealing while hiding the damage that the trap will inflict.

Think of the classic picture of a mousetrap, a piece of cheese right there for the taking. The mouse thinks to himself, "Thank God! Give us this day our daily cheese." He goes for it, then *splat!* No more mouse! Or think of some of your favorite superhero shows. The devious villain always sets a trap for the hero. What kind of trap does he use? It's usually something the hero desires or wants to protect. The hero falls for it, then the villain captures him. If you're a fan of superhero TV shows and movies, then you know there's good news: the hero always finds a way to escape! Usually, this happens with assistance from someone else (spoiler alert!). But before we go down that path, let me be clear: the truth is, traps are deceptive and disguised well. Within the traps are things we want. I know this may seem obvious, but I believe this is an overlooked reality. Traps are only an effective weapon when the enemy fills them with something desirable.

The trap of familiarity appeals to one of our greatest desires as humans: the need for safety. This isn't just my opinion. Maslow's hierarchy of needs is a psychological theory that structures our fundamental human needs. At the basic level—right after food, water, and sleep—is the need for safety and security. We desire freedom from fear. In fairness, this desire is connected to our need to feel physically safe. However, I think Maslow was on to something bigger. Presumably, our need for safety causes us to sit back in life and play it safe. We associate familiarity with security, both consciously and subconsciously. When we are familiar with something, we feel safer than when we encounter something unfamiliar. Or, so we think.

The truth is traps are deceptive. The places we think provide the most safety actually pose the greatest danger to our destinies. The misleading, false sense of security creates complacency. Traps are deceptive in their nature because the one who sets them is deceptive in his very nature. You didn't think the trap set itself, did you? Nope. It is my deep conviction that the Bible is trustworthy. It teaches us that the same one who has been setting traps since the beginning of time is still setting them now. And boy, is he decep-

> *The places we think provide the most safety actually pose the greatest danger to our destinies.*

tive! He is so deceptive that the Scripture refers to him as "the Father of Lies" (John 8:44 ESV). In that same verse, he is described as having no truth in him. Lying is a part of his very nature. It's no wonder the trap is so effective. It's been set by the Chief Deceiver! This is surely why the apostle Paul encourages us to "put on the full armor of God, [so] that you will be able to stand firm against the schemes of the devil" (Ephesians 6:11 ESV). Paul clearly tells us that the way to avoid falling into the deceptive traps of life is to cling closer to God. This is only possible when you trade in fear for faith, and you dare to venture into what may be uncomfortable. This leads us to another truth about the trap.

 ## Traps Seem Comfortable

I remember a story I once heard about a woman and a large boa constrictor, which happened to be her pet snake. The woman would play with the snake regularly, all in what she thought was good fun. Every night, the snake would cozy up with her in the bed. The following morning, she would wake up, and the snake had part of its mouth on her body. The woman thought nothing of it. After all, the snake was her pet. She played with it and cared for it. This happened for several nights consistently until one day, the woman was found to be totally consumed by the snake. All those nights, the snake had been deceptively measuring whether it could devour her.

What's the moral of the story? Don't buy a pet snake! No, I'm kidding. The moral of the story is that if you aren't careful, what you get comfortable with will consume you.

Comfortability is the by-product of familiarity and the silent killer of destiny. We should live our lives with a healthy discomfort and discontent for where we are. Let me emphasize the word *healthy!* It is possible to have an unhealthy discontent and discomfort for life and where we are. This attitude manifests itself through instability in our lives or an obsession with attaining more and more. This is contrary to how Scripture encourages us to live (Philippians 4:11–13;

> **In the spaces where we are comfortable, we are less likely to be courageous, less likely to move by faith, and less likely to trust God.**

1 Timothy 6:6–12). However, it is also true that destiny lives in the place of healthy discomfort and discontentment. The problem is the trap of familiarity, by nature, replaces these feelings with an unhealthy sense of comfort, and, well, comfort kills. In the spaces where we are comfortable, we are less likely to be courageous, less likely to move by faith, and less likely to trust God. We will never experience God's best for our lives without learning to trust him in uncomfortable situations. Our faith kicks into high gear while enduring uncomfortable situations, and it's only by faith that God is pleased with us (Hebrews 11:6).

I'm So Uncomfortable

This reminds me of my first mission trip. I received a last-minute phone call from one of my best friends on a Monday, asking if I could be in Jacmel, Haiti, two days later to preach at a conference. The missionary slated to attend fell ill and couldn't make it, so they asked me to fill in for him. Though I was pretty ecstatic about the opportunity, I was also a little anxious, not knowing what to expect.

I arrived in Port-au-Prince on Wednesday. There was someone at the airport waiting to transport me to the compound where I'd be staying for the night. We got in the car, and *whoosh!* He took off! He drove way faster than I thought was safe, and I tend to have a heavy foot, so that's saying something. On top of it all, not every road we traveled on was fully paved. The driver weaved through traffic, braked suddenly to avoid hitting cars, honked the horn, hurried those who were in his way, and swerved to avoid pedestrians walking on the street. I was so uncomfortable.

By the grace of God, we arrived at the compound. The staff told me to get some rest, for we would drive through the mountains to reach the camp the next day. The following morning I walked outside. There, smiling by the car, was the same driver. Instantly, I felt anxious.

We began our two-hour trek through the mountains. Before leaving the compound, I thought, *"Surely he'll take it slower on these mountainous roads."* The thought quickly evaporated. I'll spare you all the details of the drive, but I'll say that more than once I had thought, *"This is how the Seth Martin story ends."* I was so uncomfortable that I had felt car sick.

Again, by God's grace, we arrived at the camp. The camp was a school made up of concrete slabs with an open basketball court in the middle and classrooms surrounding it. The classrooms were enclosed spaces with desks and a doorless frame made of concrete. They took me into one of the classrooms and pointed to a mattress, telling me this was where I would be sleeping for the next four days. Still excited about the experience but nervous about the unexpected, I said, "Cool!"

My cool quickly turned cowardly. Several times, I heard interesting noises echoing through the night's silence. Bugs of all kinds landed on my body, gnawing at me. I attempted to go to the restroom in the middle of the night only to be greeted by a spider the size of my hand. After seeing it, I figured I could hold it until the morning. To top it all off, it was hot. Like, burning hot! Now, I'm sure if you are an experienced missionary, you're slightly judging and/or laughing at me, saying, "Duh, Seth, that's how mission trips are!" Fair enough, but again this was my first trip. I was learning here, so cut me some slack. Needless to say, that night, I was so uncomfortable.

However, there was a turning point. The next morning I woke up early—or should I say got up early since I never actually fell asleep. It was still pitch black outside; the sun hadn't risen yet. All of a sudden, I heard singing. The students at the camp were singing as they woke up. One of the guides explained to me that this was a normal practice. A single student in each room set an alarm, and as he or she got up, the student would begin to sing. The singing would wake up the rest of the students, and before I knew it, the whole room of campers was making a joyful noise to the Lord for another day.

Wow, talk about a gut check! I never wake up singing! Even though I have a cozy bed, a decent roof over my head, more clothes than I need, and definitely eat more food than I should, I never wake up singing, but they do. They sing even though many of these children can't afford an education, don't have parents who provide for them, and don't have running water or consistent meals to eat. Realizing this, my thought of *"I'm so uncomfortable"* turned into *"I'm so grateful!"*

While I was there, I fulfilled my assignment to preach the gospel. I preached six times in five days, and by God's grace and power, five people accepted Christ in faith. I returned home the following week exhausted yet somehow fueled by the experience. A few days later, I received a text message from the pastor who invited me on the trip. He thanked me again for traveling to Haiti to spread the gospel. The pastor then told me that one of the young ladies who accepted Christ while I was there had confessed to his wife that she was involved in prostitution. The 16-year-old had been doing so because she needed money to purchase personal hygiene products. But now that she was a follower of Jesus, she left that lifestyle behind, trusting Christ would provide for her every need.

My eyes flooded with tears. Was it worth being uncomfortable for? Yes. God not only used the uncomfortable setting to change me during that trip, but he also used me to cultivate change in someone else, which inevitably led her to follow Christ. That trip reminded me that discomfort and destiny often occupy the same space. God does his best work in us and through us in uncomfortable places. If I had never left the familiarity of my home for the uncertainty of Haiti, I would have never learned how to wake up singing. Also, a young girl may not have heard of a man named Jesus who saves.

Traps Seem Reliable

The Indiana Jones series are some of the best movies ever. It doesn't matter how much time has passed since their debut (which I wasn't even alive for). I will always love them! As I was contemplating the truth about traps, I couldn't help but think about these movies. If you're unfamiliar with them, let me bring you up to speed.

The series stars a young Harrison Ford, who plays a character named Indiana Jones. Jones is a professor of archeology by day and a treasure hunter during every other time in his life. In each film, Indiana Jones finds himself on a wild adventure in ancient temples and cities, recovering valuable, lost artifacts while avoiding bullets, spears, and booby traps. Almost without fail, Jones encounters a booby trap as he draws within inches of the artifact he's seeking.

As I was thinking about traps, the one that jumped out to me was from the third installment of the series, *Indiana Jones and the Last Crusade*. *Spoiler alert:* in the end, Indiana has to walk across a floor of stones with letters on them, stepping on just the right ones. If he steps on the wrong stone, then the bottom would fall out, and he'd plunge to his death (which almost happens). As I pondered this booby trap, I realized it was effective and potentially dangerous because all of the stones seemed equally sturdy and reliable.

Isn't this a revelation regarding the nature of traps? They always seem reliable. So it is with the trap of familiarity. The familiar areas of our lives give off the appearance of reliability and stability. We think the stones that we stand on are safe and reliable. However, once the ground falls beneath us, we quickly realize they were never reliable at all. They were just hollow and flimsy as the air we fell through on our way to the ground. I'll delve into this deeper a little later. But for now, I'll say this: the only thing truly reliable in life is the faith you place in God. No matter how reliable the place may feel, the ground could crumble. So, don't live your life playing it safe in familiar surroundings thinking it's reliable. Only your trust in God guarantees you won't fall through the air to the ground.

The truth about traps, specifically the trap of familiarity, is that they are deceptive in nature. They offer us the appearance of comfort, which

is the great enemy of fulfilling your calling in life. Comfort and familiarity seem reliable, but they will send you falling to your demise as soon
as you step into them. We need honest
introspection. We need to search our
hearts to determine whether we're staying in what is familiar out of fear or if we
are trusting God to lead us through the
unfamiliar by faith.

Are you living in fear or walking in faith?

If you are stuck in the familiar, I pray that God will strengthen your
faith to believe in him and move your feet where he wants you to go.
But before we get there, we have more to discuss. Though we understand
the nature of the trap of familiarity, there is something else you need to
learn about this trap. Familiarity presents itself in different ways in all of
our lives. Like sin in the hearts of humanity, the familiar traps look unique
in all of our lives. We can be trapped in the familiarity of a relationship,
home, job security, past success, or even moving. Yes, some of us can
become so familiar with moving from place to place that we never stay
anywhere long enough for God to use us. This is also a trap. I will unpack
these different versions of the trap throughout the next few chapters
and then encourage you to make faith moves. Let's start with the trap of
familiarity that happens at home.

CHAPTER 2
The Home Trap ←—

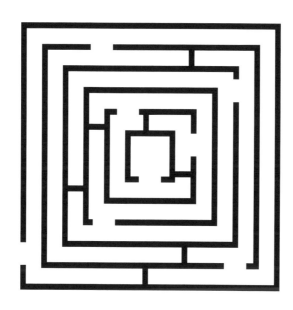

"Go from your land, your relatives,
and your father's house to the land that I will show you."

Genesis 12:1 CSB

"Pack up your bags," God said. "Kiss your family members goodbye, and leave your home.

"Where am I going, Lord?" Abram asked.

"I'll let you know on the way."

This was the very first conversation that Scripture records between God and Abram, the patriarch of the entire nation of Israel. God calls Abram (later renamed Abraham) to leave the familiarity of his home and family. Verse 4 conveys, "So Abram went."

So, what happened after that? If you're unfamiliar with the story, I'll skip to the good part for you. God did what he always does. He kept his promise! God told Abraham that if he obeyed him and stepped out of the familiar, then he would step into the favor of God. The Lord said, "I will make you into a great nation, I will bless you, I will make your name great, and you will be a blessing. I will bless those who bless you, I will curse anyone who treats you with contempt, and all the peoples on earth will be blessed through you" (Genesis 12:2–3 csb). And this is exactly what God did.

Don't believe me? Let's go down the list.

1. **I will make you into a great nation.** From Abraham, the whole nation of Israel would be born. Check!

2. **I will make your name great.** Minimally, every Christian and Jew ever has heard of Abraham, and if you haven't, you're hearing about him now in this book. It's safe to say his name is great. Check!

3. **I will bless those who bless you and curse anyone who treats you with contempt.** If you read the story of Abraham's life, you will see that God took care of those who honored him and punished those who dishonored Abraham. Check!

4. **All the peoples on earth will be blessed through you.** Do you remember how I told you the whole nation of Israel came from Abraham? Well, generations later, a whole bunch of people would

have babies, and one of those babies would be named Mary. God chose Mary to give birth to a baby named Jesus. Yes, that Jesus! Jesus would live the perfect life that we couldn't live, die the painful death we were supposed to die, and be raised from the dead on a glorious Sunday morning, proving he is indeed God. He saved the world from our sins, offering us eternal life with God if only we only believe in him. Woah! It's safe to say that all the people on earth were blessed through Abraham. All of this happened for him and through him because he made a faith move to leave the familiarity of his home and trust God to lead him.

This is what I'm trying to tell you: God's favor rests on those who have enough faith to follow him away from the familiar. We witness God's blessings in our lives when we trust God to lead the way, even if the path is away from home. This is what Abraham discovered in his life, and it's what I pray we all experience in ours.

> *God's favor rests on those who have enough faith to follow him away from the familiar.*

Can you imagine how hard this must have been for Abraham? Though the Bible doesn't give insight into Abraham's thinking, the notion of simply leaving the place that Abraham called home and the people that he called family is tough. Perhaps you're dealing with a similar situation now. You lived in the same place possibly your whole life. Your friends are there, and your family is there. You're comfortable at home, yet there is a sense that God is leading you somewhere else for a divine assignment. Perhaps it's going to college in another state. Maybe it's moving to accept a new position in another city. Or maybe it's moving to help plant a church or to become a missionary. Whatever it is, you feel a tug on your heart that God might be leading you to do something else that will cause you to leave the familiarity of your home.

I want to encourage you to take a step of faith. Don't wait for a smoke signal from God or a message in the sky made up of birds. Just do it! If you have prayed about it and you have spoken to wise consultants, don't make it hard on yourself. Trust God and make a move. Make a *faith move* like I did.

I love reading Kevin DeYoung's book called *Just Do Something*. I read it almost every year, as it is a constant reminder for me to trust God and make decisions. In his book, DeYoung says, "When it comes to most of our daily decisions, and even a lot of life's 'big' decisions, God expects and encourages us to make choices, confident that he's already determined how to fit our choices into his sovereign will." He's basically saying you can move by faith, trusting that God has already factored in how the move will affect your life. I pray that this thought liberates you from overthinking the decision. I'm encouraging you to trust God and move by faith. That means you should pray. Ask yourself, *"Will this decision glorify God in my life?"* If the answer is yes, then go for it!

Here's my call to action for you: ***Be bold enough to leave the place you call home.*** Even if you don't fully know where God will take you, trust that you will end up right where you need to be. Even if you make missteps along the way as you move—and you will—the best news is God factors in your failures, too.

 ## Be Led Away. Don't Run Away.

Now, before we move forward on making this faith move away from home, it is crucial for me to clarify who should make this move. The person who trusts God to leave home is being led away. This person is not running away. There may be someone reading this book who believes moving to another city is the solution to all of their problems. I've seen it all too many times. In fact, I'll talk about the moving trap later.

Growing up in Little Rock, Arkansas, it's funny how I heard people articulate that their lives would somehow be better if they moved to Dallas, Texas. Don't get me wrong; I love Dallas. It's perhaps my favorite southern city in the United States. Still, it is not heaven, nor is any other city on this earth. Moving to another destination to run away from your problems is not the same as being led away by God's purpose and promise.

The reality is a new place will not absolve you of your problems if you're still the same old person. Suppose you're contemplating moving because you believe life will be better somewhere else. I'd like you to consider that maybe God wants to change your character but not change your surroundings.

> *Maybe God wants to change your character and not change your surroundings.*

After being questioned about fasting, Jesus made an interesting point to a few misguided religious officials. He said, "No one puts new wine into old wineskins. Otherwise, the wine will burst the skins, and the wine is lost as well as the skins. No, new wine is put into fresh wineskins" (Mark 2:22 CSB). In context, Jesus is speaking about his ministry and the old Jewish ideology, which ultimately rejected him as the Messiah. But the principle applies to various areas of life: you don't put something new into something old or something old into something new. You wouldn't want to take a single mentality into a marriage or take a low-impact work ethic to a high-stakes job. It is almost certainly a waste when you do this. But, we all tend to do this. We must be intentional in recognizing and correcting the habits that hold us back. Perhaps God hasn't put you in a new environment because you still have some old habits, mindsets, and tendencies that need to change. Hear me, my friend: your new surroundings won't matter. If you bring your old character with you, it'll be a waste, like putting new wine in an old wine sack.

But I have good news for you: whatever is old in your life, Jesus can make new. It does not matter how long you've been dealing with the issue. It doesn't matter how long you've had the attitude, dealt with the hurt, or had the addiction. If you trust Jesus with your life, he promises to make you new. Paul, the apostle, said it like this, "Therefore, if anyone is in Christ, he is a new creation; the old has passed away, and see, the new has come!" (2 Corinthians 5:17 CSB). Jesus can take our old lives and make them new. As you ponder leaving the familiarity of home, be sure that you're being led away and not running away.

 ## Learn What to Leave Behind

On August 25, 2001, the world lost one of its brightest entertaining stars at the young age of 22 in a plane crash. Aaliyah, a famed R&B singer and actress, was killed along with eight other people soon after takeoff while the aircraft attempted to leave the Bahamas. She had just shot the music video "Rock the Boat." Eyewitnesses and professionals alike attested that it was one of the worst crashes they'd ever seen. As tragic as the crash was, perhaps even more tragic was one of the possible causes for it. One witness testified that Aaliyah's team debated with the aircraft's pilot before their departure. He tried to explain to them that the plane was overloaded. The amount of equipment, paired with the number of people on the aircraft, was going to be too much for the metal bird in the sky to handle. However, the team insisted they needed everyone, including their equipment, to be on the same flight. Tragically, the plane wouldn't make it more than 200 feet from the airstrip before it went down because it was overloaded.

Dr. Phillip Pointer, one of my mentors and the senior pastor at Saint Mark Baptist Church in Little Rock, Arkansas, tells this story in a sermon he calls "Learning What to Leave Behind." While in no way do I suggest that the crash was the fault of Aaliyah's team, I can't help but think of how differently things could have turned out if the pilot or the passengers would have made the hard decision to leave some things behind. Consequently, I believe there is a lesson to be learned from this tragedy. Like that plane, our lives are in danger of being overloaded, crashing, and burning when we continue to carry what God is commanding us to leave behind. This is imperative for us to understand, especially as we discuss leaving the familiarity of home.

Sometimes we are obedient to leave places God tells us to leave, but we don't leave people God tells us to leave. If you're going to leave the familiarity of home, you can't just leave the place; you have to be willing to leave some people behind, too. This is part of God's command to Abraham when he tells him to leave his home and go to a land that God will show him. Genesis 12:1 CSB conveys, "The Lord said to Abram: Go out from your land, **your relatives,** and your father's house" (emphasis mine). But when you examine verse 4, the writer makes a notation that sticks out. "So Abram went, as the Lord had told him, **and Lot went with him."** (emphasis mine). Dang! We were doing so well until we got to that last little phrase. While Abraham got it right in leaving the land by faith, he got it wrong in taking his nephew, Lot, with him. He was well-intentioned in taking his nephew with him. Still, God's instructions were clear: Abraham was to leave his home and his relatives behind and follow God. But, Abraham only did the former.

If this sounds familiar, it's because we all tend to do this to God. Sometimes, we partially obey God's commands or somehow attempt to make up for our disobedience. We give to the church, but we don't give the tithe (10 percent). We didn't have penetrating sex, but we performed

> *There is nothing we can give God as a substitute for our obedience.*

other sexual acts. We didn't cuss someone out, but we were still rude. In our attempts to somewhat obey God, we often use loopholes and shortcuts to partially obey his commands. But the truth is, partial obedience is still disobedience. There is nothing we can give to God as a substitute for our obedience.

Samuel, a prophet in Israel, said to Saul, a disobedient king, "Does the Lord take pleasure in burnt offerings and sacrifices as much as in obeying the Lord? Look: to obey is better than sacrifice, to pay attention is better than the fat of rams" (1 Samuel 15:22 CSB). He makes it clear that God is much more interested in you following his instructions than you trying to make up for not following them with a good deed. And when God gives us clear instructions, as he has done in his Word, it is not to be mean. It is for our own good.

I encourage you to read Genesis 13-19. But to prove my point, I will tell you that Abraham faced unnecessary dilemmas because he took Lot along. Abraham and Lot's servants argued over land. A foreign ruler captured Lot, and old Abe had to save him. Then, Lot lingered in a place when he should have left. Abraham prayed for God to spare him. God does it, but because Lot was slow to leave and he was disobedient for not going where God told him, Lot's wife died, and his daughters tricked him into sleeping with them. Sheesh! That's a drama way better than anything you will find on any of Shonda Rhimes' shows! From a macro view, it all happens because Abraham did not follow God's directions to leave his relatives behind. The good news? This hiccup did not stop or hinder God's plans for Abraham's life. Thank God he always factors in our failures! But still, the journey was a lot rockier than it probably had to be.

Like Aaliyah and Abraham, we must learn to trust God and leave some people and things behind when he leads us away. Sometimes we think we are performing an honorable deed by taking them with us. But in reality, we are doing more damage to our lives (and even to their lives) than good. So, be bold and trust that God will not only take care of you as he leads you to new places, but he will also take care of them as they stay in that place. God has a plan for both of your lives far beyond what you can comprehend, and he doesn't need your help fulfilling it. So when God is leading you out of the familiar trap, you must learn what to leave behind. Pray to God and ask yourself, *"Does this relationship, job, or mindset help me to be who God wants me to be? Is this what God wants me to do?"* Be honest. Are you more Christ-like because of them? If the answer is no, then let it go. That way, as your life takes off into the sky, you'll soar like God intended you.

 ## It's Never Too Late to Leave

One of the things I love so much about the Bible, is that God puts these seemingly minute details throughout the narratives of people's lives. These details are very important but easily overlooked if you're not careful. That's what we find in the last sentence of Genesis 12:4 CSB. If you read slowly enough, the importance of this sentence will leap out at you. It says, "Abram was seventy-five years old when he left Haran."

Just in case you missed it, allow me to help make it clear. Abraham was pretty old when God called him to leave his home and revealed his destiny to him. Even with our advances in modern medicine, 75 isn't exactly the prime years of a person's life. Yet, God pulls on the heart of this 75-year-old man and tells him to leave his home.

Abraham was 75-years-old when God revealed that he would be the father of a nation. Wow! What is God telling us? Here it is: God's usage of our lives is not determined by our age. No matter your age, it is never too late (or early) for God to use your life for greatness. It is never too late for you to trust him and step out on faith.

> **It is never too late (or early) for God to use your life for greatness.**

This news can be both exciting and daunting. It's exciting because, for a brief moment, you are filled with a ray of hope. It's not too late to move to another city, to start a business, to accept your calling, to forgive those who hurt you, to share your faith with someone, to be a good parent, or to be a faithful spouse. How exciting! All of the things you desired to do but thought were stripped away by time's passing are still on the table.

But it is also scary because it has blown up your excuses for why you shouldn't do it:

I'm not educated enough.

I didn't come from the best family.

I don't have enough money.

The mistakes I've made are too big.

Now you are left to face the reality that if you don't do it, it is because you let fear hold you back instead of allowing faith to move you forward.

I pray that you will experience God's favor in your life. I pray that you are moved by faith and not by the self-induced fear of failure. Nevertheless, I'm sure there is someone who is on edge about stepping out on faith. You're saying, "Seth, that sounds good, but there are some things you should do when you're young. I'm too old for that kind of stuff. And, it's laughable to think I can do that at my age."

Let me respond with an invitation to lean in closer: *God is not limited by time, which means your opportunities aren't limited just because you're older.* And as far as what God's calling you to do being laughable? I'll just say what God said to Sarah, Abraham's wife, after she laughed when God told her she would have a child after she passed her child-bearing age. "Is anything impossible for the Lord?" (Genesis 18:14 CSB). No matter how long you've been at home or wherever you are, Abraham teaches us it's never too late to leave and follow the Lord.

CHAPTER *3*
The Parent Trap ⟵

"'Why were you searching for me?' He asked them. 'Didn't you
know that it is was necessary for me to be in my Father's house?'
But they did not understand what he said to them."

Luke 2:49–50 CSB

Do you remember the movie *The Parent Trap?* There were two versions: the original, made in 1961, and the more recent, made in 1998. I grew up with the 1998 version. I'm feeling kind of old as I write this, realizing that 1998 was over 20 years ago. Anyway, the movie was about twin sisters separated at birth after their parent's heated divorce. To make things easier on their daughters, the parents separated the twins: one girl lived with the mother while the other lived with the father. The girls later, by chance, meet one another and then hatch a plan to reunite the divorced lovers. It was a pretty good movie. The truth is this movie has nothing to do with this chapter. It just felt appropriate to mention it because the chapter is called *The Parent Trap,* and so was the movie. Ha! It's okay if you didn't laugh. This is one of my dad jokes. My wife thinks I'm corny, too.

A more appropriate movie to illustrate the point of this chapter would be the classic comedy *The Waterboy* starring Adam Sandler. In the film, Bobby Boucher, Sandler's character, is a college-aged country boy living in Louisiana. He obsesses over quality water while serving as the waterboy for his hometown's college football team.

> *While often well-intentioned, parents can, at times, be roadblocks to a child's growth and development.*

After being bullied by some of the players, he gets fed up and lays one of them out, revealing his natural ability to play football. However, there is one small problem: the waterboy is also a mama's boy. Bobby has an overprotective mother who, out of her own insecurities, attempts to keep Bobby from playing football, falling in love, or even getting an education. Throughout the movie, this young man wrestles with trying not to disappoint his mama while attempting to pursue his destiny. This point speaks more to the heart of this chapter. It points to the reality that parents can become a trap in our lives, inhibiting us from reaching our God-given destiny. For most people prior to marriage, there is no one on the earth that knows them better than their parents. While often well-intentioned, parents can, at times, be roadblocks to a child's growth and development.

If they aren't careful, familiarity and parental influence can hinder the children's destiny instead of helping it.

At 12-years-old, I was in the seventh grade at Horace Mann Middle School. I can only recall two things from that time. One, I had a science teacher named Mr. Johnson, who I didn't like very much. But now that I'm older, I respect him greatly because he was the only African-American male teacher I had until I reached college. I realize now that he was hard on me because he didn't want to see a young black boy become a statistic. The other thing I recall is that I had a crush on a girl named Latika Johnson. She was not related to Mr. Johnson. Though I liked Latika, unfortunately, she didn't like me back. Still, she was nice to me, so I held out hope that one day she'd change her mind.

Basically, at age 12, my life consisted of two things: trying to survive Mr. Johnson's class and hoping Latika Johnson would someday realize that I was the guy for her. It was a pretty typical middle school experience. I'm sure if you reflected on your experience as a 12-year-old, it was probably something similar. You probably had your first crushes, had a teacher you didn't care for, wanted to hang out with your friends all the time, and that was about it. You kept it light; nothing too serious. You probably weren't concerned about exploring and explaining theology or excavating the great love of God. No, if you were like me, you were just trying to understand basic biology, not theology. You were busy building chemistry with your first love, and not thinking about God's great love. But Jesus did.

At age 12, Jesus was already understanding, thinking, and explaining the greatness of God to those older than him. Luke 2:41-50 gives us insight into Jesus' incredible commitment to his divine assignment and the tension it caused between him and his parents. The Scriptures convey that every year, his family went to Jerusalem to celebrate the Passover festival, a Jewish holiday celebrating God's faithfulness to the Jews while they were enslaved in Egypt. The book of Exodus notes that the Jews obeyed God's instructions, so the death angel passed over them when it came as a final plague on Pharaoh and Egypt. In light of this reality, those of Jewish descent would annually celebrate the greatness of God during the Passover festival. Out of all the years that Jesus and his parents attended the Passover festival, there is one that stands out: the year that

Mary and Joseph left Jesus behind after the festival concluded. His parents traveled back to Jerusalem, where Mary found him teaching in the temple.

This story is a noteworthy account for several reasons. For one, it is the only Scripture that speaks explicitly about the childhood of Jesus. Other than this passage, the Scripture does not explicitly elaborate on the upbringing of Christ. We read about his birth, then we jump to the beginning of his public ministry at the age of 30, following him all the way until his resurrection and ascension into heaven. Secondly, it points to Jesus' divine otherness at an early age, evidenced by his unique ability to understand and explain the Scripture as one with great authority. He wasn't the 12-year-old catching a few Z's while the pastor preached, nor was he playing games on his iPad during the worship service. Instead, Luke 2:46-47 CSB says, "After three days they found him in the temple sitting among the teachers, listening to them and asking them questions. And all who heard him were astounded at his understanding and his answers." He was focused and engaged, answering questions that astounded the teachers in the temple. It showed his sovereign uniqueness. But more importantly, for the context of this chapter, this passage of Scripture shows us the tension of living out our calling and dealing with the parent trap. While the teachers were amazed by his answers, his parents were aggravated, unaware of his whereabouts.

Home Alone

My favorite movie to watch around the holidays is *Home Alone 2: Lost in New York,* starring Macaulay Culkin. As I write, I'm reminded of that scene when the McCallister's arrive at the baggage claim area in the airport. As they're passing out luggage, suddenly, the family realizes that Macaulay Culkin's character, Kevin, wasn't there. They'd left him home alone, again. Then his mother screams, "KEVIN!" and faints.

Mary probably felt this way after leaving the Passover festival, realizing that she had just left the Savior behind in Jerusalem. The Scripture tells us they assumed he was somewhere among the group as they traveled together. It took them a whole day to realize that he wasn't riding in someone else's car, figuratively speaking. Don't judge them too harshly. We've all misplaced a kid before, right? I imagine Mary hit Joseph on the shoulder, saying, "It was your turn to check on him." And old Joe responded, " He's only my stepson. I thought you knew where he was." Flash-sideways: 12-year-old Jesus was in the temple listening, inquiring, and answering the teacher's questions as they studied the Scripture. The Savior was in the temple focused on his Father's business, fulfilling his divine calling to save humanity. He was so focused that he didn't even flinch when his family's caravan pulled out and headed home.

After they had realized he was missing, Joseph and Mary finally found Jesus three days later. I speculate that they were filled with a sense of relief that Jesus was okay. But you don't have to guess what else they were thinking. Different biblical translations describe their feelings as hurt, upset, overwhelmed, anxious, and astonished. They were pretty disappointed, to say the least. This is evident in their question to Jesus once they found him. "Son, why have you treated us like this? Your father and I have been anxiously searching for you" (Luke 2:48 CSB). To which, Jesus replies, "Why were you searching for me? Didn't you know that it was necessary for me to be in my Father's house?"

Jesus' response seems bold. There is no way I would've gotten away with a response like that, not with the type of parents I grew up with! The Scripture would've read, "Seth responded, 'Why were you searching for me?' And Seth died that day in the temple at the hands of his parents." Only the Savior of the world can make a statement like that to his parents after he's been missing for three days!

All jokes aside, this exchange shows us what happens to all of us at some point in our lives. Jesus wasn't being disrespectful in his response, nor was he trying to worry his parents. He was just sure of his purpose. He knew where he was supposed to be and exactly when he was supposed to be there. Jesus is God, completely all-knowing. Fully man, yet somehow still fully God. Answering questions and astonishing those who listened while studying in the temple was a part of God's divine plan to reveal himself to others and save the world. Now, we aren't Jesus. But God has uniquely gifted all of us with a purpose. You have an assignment to complete while on this earth that's specifically designed just for you. There is no one else that has been made, is made, or will be made to do the things God has called you to do. In order to do it, you have to be exactly where God has called you to be. Like Jesus, you have to know where you need to fulfill your assignment. Then, you need faith to get there, even if it means disappointing those who know you because they don't understand.

 ## Parents Just Don't Understand

Well parents are the same no matter the time nor place.
So to you, all the kids all across the land,
Take it from me, parents just don't understand.

Jesus was probably humming these lines of the song "Parents Just Don't Understand" in his head that day in the temple. Long before the birth of Will Smith and DJ Jazzy Jeff, Jesus was probably thinking through the words of this anthem as he explained the necessity for him to be in the temple that day. Jesus explains that this is a part of God's plan for his life.

Check out the last line of the narrative in Luke 2:50 csb: "But they did not understand what He said to them." Translation: his parents just didn't understand.

I would like to challenge a common belief among families. That is, the idea that parents know their children better than the child or anyone else that knows them. While I understand and agree that parents may have more insight into their children's lives than others, I disagree that they know them better than anyone. Practically speaking, children's thoughts and behaviors change in ways that alter their lives completely as they are exposed to people and experiences, often beyond the parent's ability and knowledge. But spiritually speaking, which is what I'm more interested in discussing, no one knows a person better than God, not even the parent. While parents may be the agent through which children are created, they are not the creators. God alone is responsible for the creation of every human being. Therefore, he alone is fully aware of their purpose. As great and insightful as parents may be, they can't claim full awareness of what God is doing in their kids' lives. The truth is, parents are watching their children's lives unfold for the first time just like the child is.

This is why I love the example of Samson's parents in Judges 13. God told Samson's parents that they would have a son who would play a pivotal role in saving Israel, God's chosen people. God gives his mother clear instructions about how to rear the child. But then, the father, Manoah, asks God for even more clarity. Here are two of his prayers: "Teach us what we are to do with the child who will be born" (vs. 8, ESV) and "What is to be this child's manner of life and mission" (vs. 12, ESV). I love that Manoah and his wife knew that even though their son was conceived through them, he was created by God. And only the Creator can determine the destiny of the creation. This is why every person has to look to God alone to understand who he's created them to be. Every parent should pray to God for guidance so the child will be nurtured in alignment with God's will.

> *Every parent should pray to God for guidance so the child will be nurtured in alignment with God's will.*

Now, I must add that God and life experience give parents wisdom that children have not yet attained. So, it is never a bad idea to listen to the counsel of parents and other older, influential people in your life on significant matters. Furthermore, Scripture is clear that there is safety in the multitude of counselors (Proverbs 15:22).

However, there comes a point when it is no longer the parent's responsibility to lead a child. Instead, the child must be guided by their own relationship with God (Proverbs 22:6–8). I like how one of my best friends, Peter Williams, says it: "We must be humble enough to accept advice, but trust God enough to make our own decisions." So you see, it is a tension to manage, not a problem to solve. You should listen to the counsel of others, but ultimately, make your decision and take responsibility for the decision you make.

To be clear, I am not saying that you shouldn't listen to your parents because they don't understand you. I am saying that only God fully understands what he is doing in your life. There will come a time when the steps God calls for you are strange to everyone around you, even those who conceived you. My biological parents, father in the ministry, brothers in the ministry, and pretty much all of my family thought I was crazy for moving to Minnesota to start a church. But I was sure this was where God was leading me. I never imagined we'd be here when something as heinous as George Floyd's murder happened. But it was strangely affirming that God sent me here for a time such as this. My entire family admits that now.

If you are a parent reading this book, understand that you won't always accurately interpret the steps God is leading your children to take. Trust that you have raised them to know God's leading for themselves. I'm a young parent. My oldest, Zoe, was almost 2-years-old and my youngest, Simone, was only 2-months-old when I started writing this book. Not only do I pray for them every day, but I also pray for myself as their dad. I won't always understand what God is doing in their life, even if I did help make them. But just like I've had to do in my own life, I have to trust them to go where God is leading them, even when I don't understand.

 ## Moving Forward

I have two calls to action in this chapter: one is directed towards those who are making decisions about the next steps in their journey, and the other is for the parent of the children making those decisions. First, be bold enough to be led by God to go to the place he is calling you to go, even if it means disappointing your parents. Second, for the parent, trust God enough to lead your children where they should go and pray that you have raised them to be led by God.

I'm sure someone is reading this book and your parents are pushing you to do one thing, but you prayed and felt God was leading you to do another. I'm not telling you to trust your gut; I'm telling you to trust God. God has given you a purpose, and he placed a calling on your life. You have reached the place where God will lead you. By this point, you are not led by your parent's advice. After all, God will not hold your parents responsible for the things you didn't accomplish. He called **you** to do it. At heaven's gates, you will be held accountable for everything you did and didn't do. You will be alone. You won't be allowed to blame your parents for the decisions you didn't make that you were supposed to make. So, leave the familiar and don't allow your parents to convince you to stay in it. Reach your fullest potential and be who God has called you to be. Don't get stuck in the parent trap.

Parents, trust that you have taught your children well and that God is leading them now. You trained them well. Trust that they won't depart from it. Don't be a parent trap. Let God take the lead, even when you don't understand.

CHAPTER 4
Relationship Blocks ⟵

"So Lot went out and spoke to his sons-in-law,
who were going to marry his daughters.
'Get up,' he said. 'Get out of this place,
for the Lord is about to destroy the city!'
But his sons-in-law thought he was joking."

Genesis 19:14 CSB

Relationships are amazing and powerful. They have the opportunity to help us unlock our fullest potential while simultaneously having the greatest potential to stifle it. In his book "The Power of the Other," Dr. Henry Cloud masterfully outlines how the right types of relationships boost our performance in life beyond what we think is possible. The wrong types of relationships are emotionally and mentally draining and often cause us to lose confidence and live beneath our potential. Some relationships can be roadblocks to you walking in your purpose. If you are reading this book, you have lived long enough to discover that people in your life have a profound impact on you. That isn't a new revelation, nor does it need to be expounded upon at length. Instead, I want to focus on why we stay in those relationships that are so draining to our lives. I believe it comes down to one word. You've probably guessed it by now: familiarity.

For some of us, we get trapped in the familiarity of relationships that are toxic to our lives. I say "we" because it has happened to me. It can happen to anyone, and I suspect it has happened to everyone to some degree or another. In fact, I can recall several times when various ladies trapped in toxic relationships came to me for advice. I would ask why they felt obligated to stay. They were beautiful, young, and smart. Surely, they could find someone else. But familiarity kept them from moving their feet. Even if the relationship was toxic, they feared leaving the known, for the unknown. Or, they clung to the possibility that they could somehow help this person become better.

I can also quickly recall examples of brothers I've known in my life. Good, strong, yet fearful men. I say "fearful" because, too often, when faced with opportunities to rid themselves of people who were negatively impacting them, they shutter at the thought of being negatively labeled after standing up for themselves. They decide not to leave a place and pursue their dreams because they are comfortable being in an intimate relationship or connecting with the friends they have around them.

The trap of relational familiarity can happen to anyone: men and women, young and old, black or white, or immature and even mature believers. In fact, there is a narrative in the Scripture that sheds some light on this reality. It includes a person named Lot, Abraham's nephew, who we discussed earlier.

The story of God's destruction of Sodom is one of the more interesting stories in Scripture. God destroys an entire city because of its wickedness, found in multiple forms. However, God rescues Lot, a man of righteous character, and his family before its destruction. He sent angels to Lot to warn him of the city's impending doom. The angels encouraged Lot to leave with his family. The part of the story that stands out for me is found in Genesis 19:15-16 CSB. "At daybreak, the angels urged Lot on: 'Get up! Take your wife and your two daughters who are here, or you will be swept away in the punishment of the city.' But he hesitated." This is borderline insane! Two angels show up on Lot's doorstep and tell him to leave the city because it's going to be destroyed, and he's sticking around, hesitating to move.

Honestly, as bad as I want to judge Lot and his family, how many times has God sent us warnings to leave a situation? We could face negative consequences, yet we stayed. There are so many reasons Lot may have lingered even when God was calling him to leave. Maybe he didn't want to leave his possessions. It could have been that he was skeptical. But there is another possibility that stands out to me, which is relevant to this chapter. It wasn't simply about leaving his possessions. I have a hunch that Lot didn't want to leave some people behind. The Scripture tells us that Lot told his sons-in-law what God had said, but they thought he was joking (Genesis 19:14). He couldn't persuade them to leave. It is possible Lot lingered because he didn't want to leave those with whom he had a relationship. However, they didn't have the same calling God placed on Lot's life. He fell into the relationship trap. He almost allowed his relationships to hold him back from where God was calling him to go.

We all live in the danger of allowing toxic relationships to keep us from our purpose. You may be in this type of relationship with a boyfriend, a girlfriend, or just a friend as I speak. All of the signs are there. You constantly feel emotionally drained by the relationship. The wise people in your life are against the relationship or friendship. You feel further, not closer to God. You may have fleeting moments of fun, but you're more drained than enriched by the relationship. If that's you, my encouragement to you is to be bold enough to pursue your God-given destiny regardless of what others are doing or how it might alter the relationship.

Two Points of Clarity

Now, let me be clear. If you are married, this does not apply to your spouse. I am not saying you have permission to leave your spouse for what you perceive to be God's calling. God honors marriage and hates divorce (Hebrews 13:4; Malachi 2:16). Therefore, God will not call you to leave your spouse no matter the circumstance, barring you're not in danger. If you think God is telling you to leave your spouse to pursue your purpose, allow me to speak on God's behalf and tell you that it is not him saying that. When you get married, the Bible is clear that two flesh becomes one (Genesis 2:23-24). Therefore, whatever purpose you have in your life includes both the husband and the wife. There should be unity and agreement in pursuing it.

However, if you are simply dating a person, this does not apply to you. Since you are not married and you are still seen as single in the eyes of God, your first responsibility is not to that person. Rather, the majority of your focus should be serving God, which means going wherever he may send you. Scripture is clear that single people (not married) have the advantage of devoting their full attention to honoring God (1 Corinthians 7:32-34). This should be your focus if you are dating, courting, or "talking" to someone before you get married. During this season, do not allow your relationship to hold you back from your God-given destiny, preventing you from reaching your full potential.

Also, I am not saying that you must abandon your relationships and friendships to pursue who God is calling you to be. One of the great advantages of the age we live in is that advances in modern technology allow us to stay connected with people even from afar. It is possible for you to leave familiar territory and live up to your potential while staying in contact with people. Remember,

> *Some relationships are seasonal. Some will end as you pursue your destiny while others transcend distance, time, and seasons.*

some relationships are seasonal. Some will end as you pursue your destiny while others transcend distance, time, and seasons. I won't lie and tell you that some relationships won't change or be lost. This old saying is true: "Some friends are in your life for a reason. Some friends are in your life for a season." However, let me assure you that the relationships that will be lost are supposed to be lost; and the ones that are supposed to remain will remain. It does not catch God off guard when people leave or stay in your life. That being said, people will wrestle with two realities before they become bold enough to escape the trap of relationships.

REALITY #1: You Can't Save Anybody

I'm thinking about creating a T-shirt that says, "Jesus saves, I don't." Now, before you think I'm being mean, hear me out. It has a dual meaning for me. First, it communicates a clear message to others that it is not my job, nor is it within my power to save you from situations. I'm establishing boundaries. Second, this serves as a reminder to myself that I am not the Savior. This point is the most important to me. We all need reminders like that, especially if we are in a ministry or seen as the dependable person in a relationship. Those of us who work with people or are seen as the dependable ones in our families have a tendency to try and save others from situations or rescue them from challenging circumstances. There is a false sense of moral obligation that we must deliver others from their issues. But the reality is, saving people is not within our abilities. You can't even save yourself from harsh circumstances and situations, let alone your sin. It is foolish and even borderline arrogant to believe you can save someone else.

But we try, don't we? We try to persuade the person to be better. We try to deliver them from their addictions. We try to love them until they respect us. We fight, strain, and exhaust ourselves attempting to change others, only to find ourselves emotionally exhausted and disappointed. The reality is none of us can change or save anyone from their circumstances or attitudes. The decision solely rests on them. As it regards other people, the only decision we can make is whether or not we will keep them in our lives.

We are not responsible for other people's lives and the fulfillment of their purpose. We can only control how we respond to God's calling.

Lot learned this lesson by experience. Genesis 19:14 tells us that Lot told his sons-in-law that God would destroy the city, but they thought he was joking. So, they stayed behind. The sons-in-law did not escape, so they were killed in the city. Can you imagine how hard that must've been for Lot? He knew that their lives were in danger. If they didn't make a radical shift and leave the city, they would die. This can be a similar scene in our lives. We see the path of destruction our friends and family are heading down, so we desperately plead that they would change and turn from it.

This scene with Lot and his sons-in-law is a daunting parallel to what happens when Christians share the Gospel and the sad reality of the outcome when others don't receive it. We know that Jesus is God. He is begging for you to leave your sin and escape into his arms. Otherwise, sin will destroy you, and you will be eternally cut off from God. Unfortunately, like Lot's sons-in-law, some people think this isn't something to take seriously. Jesus describes what we are to do when this happens. He says, "If anyone does not welcome you or listen to your words, shake the dust off your feet when you leave that house or town" (Matthew 10:14 CSB). For some relationships, this is what we must do.

Reality #2: You Can Shake Them Off

I remember when I played football in middle school. One time, I took the worst hit ever from my friend Jaalen Watkins. He was such a skilled player and an advanced athlete, and he was much bigger and better than I was. One day at practice, they decided to put me on offense for some reason. You see, I was usually a cornerback (a defensive position), and Jaalen was normally a running back (an offensive position). But for whatever reason, they decided that day to switch us. I got the ball, and WHACK! The next thing I knew, I was getting up off the ground, pain coursing through my body, and my coach was screaming at me, "Shake it off!" Somehow, he wanted me to figure out a way to shake off the pain. I had a tough time shaking that kind of pain off. In fact, I don't know how possible it is to shake off physical pain, especially from a concussion, which we later discovered I had. However, it is possible to shake off people.

Avoiding relationship roadblocks requires us to learn how to shake off people. This isn't just post-modern secular human wisdom. It is an eternal truth rooted in biblical teaching. The writer of proverbs repeatedly encourages readers to be mindful and leave the company of people who aren't following God (Proverbs 13:20; 14:7; 22:24-25). Jesus notes a specific circumstance when this instruction should be applied. While teaching his disciples about sharing the Gospel, he instructs them to "shake the dust off your feet" if the people won't receive or listen to them. His point is clear: move on from those people. He discourages them from wasting more time because others will receive what they have to share. The disciples follow Jesus' command in Acts 13:51. While every person is made in the image of God and worthy of human dignity, not every person is of God. Escaping the trap of familiarity means understanding which people to sow into and which people to shake off. Some people are not worthy of partaking in your God-given destiny.

 ## Don't Settle

I've shared a lot about Lot (get it?). But allow me to share with you a little more about Lot. (See what I did there? I kill myself.)

Anyway, Lot's story becomes even more interesting. He does leave Sodom and escape its destruction. However, he doesn't go where God instructs him to go. The angels tell him to flee to the hills, but fear keeps Lot from living God's path. Instead, he requests to settle in a place called Zoar, which he thinks is a more realistic journey. God obliges his request, but it comes at a cost. Lot's wife is killed in Zoar. This tragedy sends ripples through their family and results in some less than appropriate behavior from his daughters later on. But lest we get too distracted, note that these things, in part at least, would've been avoided had Lot believed in God and his plan, rather than settling for something else.

I'm trying to free you from the spirit of settling in your life. Most people don't escape the traps of life (especially the relationship trap) because they question whether God has better for them. God has already declared he does. God has better friends for you, better boyfriends/girlfriends, and better confidants for you. Expect for God to align you with people that will encourage you, support you, and push you towards your God-given destiny. ***Don't settle for the people God has called you to shake off.***

 ## The Other Side of the Relational Trap

Lest it sounds all doom and gloom—as if I'm telling you to avoid all of your friends—let me offer some insights into what a healthy relationship looks like. Some relationships transcend seasons, time, and distance. There will be people who stay in your life from afar as you leave the familiar and go pursue what God has for you. You will recognize these people by a few characteristics.

1.   *They encourage you.*

Supportive friends push you to be who God has called you to be. They don't envy what God is doing in your life. They are genuinely proud of you and happy that God has placed such a unique destiny in front of you. They don't want to do anything to stand in the way of that purpose. They trust that God will take care of you, and they trust whatever plan he has for your relationship/friendship. By the way, these are not only characteristics to look for in others, but they are also characteristics to aspire to for ourselves.

A great example of this is a man named Jonathan. He was the son of Saul, the first king of Israel, and the rightful heir to the throne. But God had other plans. God had appointed and subsequently anointed David to be the next king. Jonathan was more than okay with that. In fact, he would encourage David on his path to the throne (1 Samuel 23:16).

2.   *They understand your life has a purpose.*

These friends are pursuing their own God-given purpose, and they are inspired by how you are pursuing yours. In fact, beneficial friends that stay in your life are people who have something going for themselves as well. These people aren't so consumed with your relationship that they're oblivious to the reality that God has big plans for them as well. They are fully aware that just as God has given you the capacity to impact the world, he has done the same for them. Therefore, even though you may be parting ways towards different paths, they are okay with it because you are both heading toward the same destination.

3. **They don't allow external factors to change the nature of your friendship.**

These friends don't let what is going on outside affect how they feel about you on the inside. They aren't moved by the constantly shifting landscape of life. Even distance and time don't change the foundation of your relationship. Children believe that to be friends, you must see or talk to one another every day. If you do speak or see your friends every day, that's great! However, maturity says if you don't, that doesn't make your friendship any less powerful.

One of my best friends, Pastor Andre Kirkland, lives in Fort Worth, Texas. My wife and I reside in Minneapolis, Minnesota, and before that, we lived in Little Rock, Arkansas, and Hampton, Virginia. I have actually never lived in the same place as my best friend. He has a wife, a child, and a full-time ministry. I am also married, have children, and have a full-time ministry. There is just no way we can speak or see each other all the time. However, when the rubber meets the road, you can bet that's who I'm calling. He has been there in some of the darkest moments of my life. Time, distance, and seasonal changes haven't destroyed our friendship. Likewise, other people who God has called to be in your life won't disintegrate your special friendship either.

4. **They aren't insecure.**

They aren't intimidated by new relationships in your life or scared of what may happen to your relationship as a result. These people are comfortable with you forming new relationships. They trust that God knows what is best for you regardless of the outcome of your relationship. They aren't worried about who was in your life first. They just want to witness God's best in your life and nothing more. And if that means that their relationship with you changes or ends, then it is okay because they trust that God knows best.

Relationships are the most important thing in life. Your most important one is with Jesus, which is never-ending. We must understand that human relationships can be and often are seasonal. God allows people to come into our lives, but we must allow him to remove them as well. God often changes your circles when he moves you to new places. Don't let the familiarity of certain relationships cause you to miss doing what God wants you to do. You may be weighing in your heart whether you are engaged in healthy relationships and whether God wants you to be in them during the next stages in your journey. Well, if this chapter has been speaking to you, hear me when I say this: don't get trapped in relationships or friendships that keep you from reaching your fullest potential. Don't let the plane of your life crash because you're carrying extra baggage. Learn to leave some people behind; it's what's best for you and for them.

Though I was greatly tempted, I was blessed to not get stuck in this trap. It was challenging to escape. Unfortunately, I know so many people who have. People who were smarter than me, more gifted than me, and maybe even had more potential to impact the world than me had allowed familiarity to trap them. Young ladies became pregnant early by men they're no longer dating or even speak to. Others allowed friends to hold them back from being the best they could be. Now, they're no longer friends with these people. These people find themselves attempting to make the best of it while being in a place they were never meant to stay. That won't be your story! If it has been you up until this point, then you're about to change the narrative. Remember, it's never too late to escape the trap!

God will remove some friendships and intimate relationships in your life. Some relationships he will preserve, while he others he will remove. Let them go. Whether the former or the latter, don't get caught in the trap. Make a faith move. Be bold enough to shake off those who are a hindrance to your spiritual development. Trust that God knows the right people to place in your life for where your purpose is taking you. Be bold enough to pursue your God-given destiny regardless of how it might alter your relationships.

CHAPTER 5
The Moving Trap ←

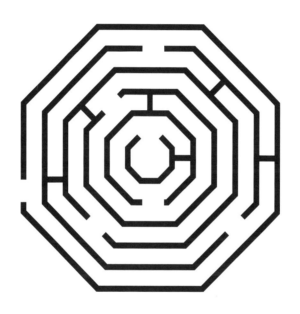

**"'Can anything good come out of Nazareth?'
Nathanael asked him."**

John 1:46 CSB

If I Can Just Make it to...

I told you about Lot's trouble in Sodom, but I never mentioned how he got there in the first place. Back in Genesis 13, in between Abraham taking Lot with him and Lot ending up in Sodom, a conflict materialized between the two. After leaving their home country and a short stint in Egypt, they found themselves living together in an area between Bethel and Ai. The Bible tells us that both Abraham and Lot possessed livestock. But the problem was they had more livestock together than they had land that could contain them. In humility and selflessness, Abraham allows Lot to choose his land first, any place in their sight. Lot's choice ultimately puts him in a compromised position.

> "Lot took a long look at the fertile plains of the Jordan Valley in the direction of Zoar. The whole area was well watered everywhere, like the garden of the Lord or the beautiful land of Egypt. (This was before the Lord destroyed Sodom and Gomorrah.) Lot chose for himself the whole Jordan Valley to the east of them. He went there with his flocks and servants and parted company with his uncle Abram. So Abram settled in the land of Canaan, and Lot moved his tent to a place near Sodom and settled among the cities of the plain. But the people of the area were extremely wicked and constantly sinned against the Lord." —Genesis 13:10–13 NLT

Lot assumed the area he chose was more prosperous because it seemed to have more desirable resources. However, sometimes what appears to be prosperous by our own understanding will get us closer to sin than we ever intended. This is what happened to Lot. He became a righteous man living in an unrighteous land. He picked a place he thought would bring him everything he wanted, but instead, it just moved him closer to sin.

I mentioned earlier that I'm from Little Rock, Arkansas. Despite public perception from people outside of the state, it is not a bad place to live. In fact, I'd argue it can be one of the better places to raise a family.

I no longer live there not because it's a bad place, but rather because God called me to go somewhere else. Now, if you asked someone else who is from there, they might offer a totally different perspective. Some natives believe that Little Rock is a confining city in a restrictive region. A suffocating surrounding where nothing flourishes. A city that is filled with people who have minimal aspirations for themselves other than earning more money to spend on indulgences. I'd be willing to bet that most of the people who adopted this perspective have a desire to escape to another city. If you're from Little Rock, it's not uncommon to want to move to either Dallas or Atlanta. However, in Minneapolis, where I currently live, people desire to escape to Chicago, Las Vegas, or anywhere warmer. I understand their desire for warmth. Winters in Little Rock are much milder than in Minneapolis.

Regardless of the city, some of us believe, like Lot, that if we can make it to whatever city we deem to be more prosperous, our lives will change for the better. We think, *"If I can just get to the next city or job, or neighborhood where other people appear to be thriving, I will thrive too."* This mindset leads us to move from city to city, neighborhood to neighborhood, career to career, searching for satisfaction. Chances are you know someone like this, or you read this paragraph and slowly realized this is an issue you have. Either way, the person who always believes success is found in something new may suffer from the ***moving trap.*** Like all of the traps I have discussed, this is a trap of the enemy. He is just trying to get you to fall in love with one of the sneakiest familiarity traps of all.

 ## The Paradox

The word "paradox" is a statement or proposition that seems self-contradictory or absurd. But in reality, it expresses a possible truth. I think that word best sums up what I've identified as the moving trap. The moving trap is when people develop an unhealthy familiarity with the unfamiliar. They become comfortable with their ever-changing surroundings, but not in a good way. The constant changing of their surroundings isn't due to their natural transitions in life or faith moves. Instead, they are attempting to manipulate their lives into success. They are striving to change their status without undergoing a change within themselves. They believe that their lack of advancement in life is connected to their physical surroundings.

I want to encourage you to see how constant sporadic movement from one place to another is a trap that will keep you from reaching your God-given destiny. As paradoxical as it seems, sometimes it takes more faith to stay where you are than it does to move to somewhere new. Perhaps that is what God is saying to you through this chapter. Stay where you are, but allow God to change who you are. He wants you to learn that your potential is not defined by your city. It is defined by your character. It's not about where you live. It is about how you live. If you need proof, nobody serves as a better case study than Jesus.

 ## Can Anything Good Come from Nazareth?

If you're a believer in Jesus Christ, when you think of Jesus, you think of perfection. You think of royalty. You think of his miracles, the cross, and his resurrection. You think about him saving you. If you're not a believer, but you still concede that Jesus was a real person who lived and died (as almost all credible scholars do), then you may at least think of Jesus as a cool rabbi. He made such an impact on the world that he's still being talked about 2000 years after his death. Whether you believe Jesus is God or just believe he was a good dude, we all have to admit he's impressive.

While the whole world is impressed by him in some way, it is funny how the place he came from was unimpressive. In fact, it was so unimpressive, one of the 12 disciples had to get over where Jesus was from before he could come to grips with the reality that he was the Messiah.

The apostle John gave us some insight into this quick exchange. Jesus just stepped onto the scene, engaging in public ministry. A man named Phillip meets and subsequently begins to follow him. Then, exemplifying the surest sign that he truly believes in Jesus, Phillip goes and tells his friend, Nathanael, that he had found the Messiah. But upon hearing where the Messiah came from, Nathanael was thrown off. Phillip tells him, "We have found Him of whom Moses in the Law and also the prophets wrote,

Jesus of **Nazareth,** the son of Joseph" (John 1:45 NKJV, emphasis mine). Nathanael responds, "Can anything good come out of Nazareth?" (vs. 46).

Nazareth was about as unimpressive a town as you could imagine. Irrefutably less impressive than any city I've ever lived in. This city was so unremarkable that it isn't even mentioned in Old Testament writings. Trade routes went near the village, but no major roads led to or from Nazareth. It wasn't a village considered worthy of knowing or mentioning by Jews, which is why Nathanael asked the question, "Can anything good come from there?" Now, the word "good" that he uses in the original language doesn't solely relate to morals. It also conveys the idea of something being beneficial. Nathanael's questions could be more relevantly communicated, "Can anything of significance come from Nazareth?"

With more truth propelling the answer than ever before, Jesus' life, death, and resurrection all scream YES! The most significant, beneficial, and righteous person ever came from Nazareth. Salvation came from Nazareth. Peace came from Nazareth. Healing came from Nazareth. Joy came from Nazareth. Love came from Nazareth. Forgiveness came from Nazareth. Eternal life came from Nazareth. Jesus came from Nazareth. From a place not important enough to have a major highway came the only highway to heaven. Through this reality, Jesus teaches us the invaluable lesson that an environment doesn't have to dictate your value. Fulfilling the purpose and plan God has placed on your life is not about where you are; it is about who you are. It is not about your surroundings; it is about your decisions. It's not about the area; it's about your anointing. The good news is God doesn't limit the anointing on your life by your dwelling place.

 ## Get Egypt Out of You

I heard a story recently about how elephants are trained in the circus. Soon after they are born, a shackle attached to their leg is tied to a wooden stake in the ground. Every time they pull too hard, the chain around their leg sinks deeper into their skin, causing cuts and bruises. Eventually, they no longer attempt to pull away from the stake because they anticipate the pain it will cause. However, the most unfortunate and cruel damage done as a result of this training is not the physical pain but the psychological paralysis it causes. Those baby elephants grow up with a chain still attached to their leg, tied to the same small stake planted in the ground. The smallest full-grown elephant weighs about 5000 pounds and can easily carry 600 pounds. Yet because they were trained to expect pain when they pull from the stake, they believe they aren't free. It is sad because the elephant doesn't know its own strength. With a slight tug, they could be free. Nevertheless, it stays because although its body is ready for freedom, its mind is not.

The same could be said for the people of Israel at a point in its history. After God delivers them from the grip of Pharaoh, the people of Israel embarked on what should have been a short journey from Egypt to Canaan. This was the promised land God intended to give them. Yet during their voyage, something became clear about this recently liberated nation: their bodies were free from Egypt, but their minds were still there. Scattered throughout the book of Exodus and Deuteronomy is evidence of Israel's inherent fear. The same fear that caused Israel to question God in Egypt was the same fear that caused them to question whether he would lead them to the promised land. They were delivered, but they still had doubts, and they were disobedient. Therefore, the issue was not the place. The issue was the people.

What most people miss is that God is far more interested in changing your character than he is changing your circumstances. A Christ-like character will allow you to have joy and fulfill your purpose even in hellacious circumstances. I dare to be bold and say that it doesn't matter where you live. What matters is whether you are allowing God to mold your character. When you allow God to shape your character, it won't matter if you're in Egypt, the wilderness, or the promised land. You will still trust God. It won't matter if you're in Little Rock, Dallas, Memphis, or Minneapolis. You will still trust God and give him your best. What's the payoff? You will experience God's best in your life not because you were in the right city but because you lived a life submitted to Christ. You will be blessed not because of the area but because you had the right attitude. You will have peace not because of the city where you reside but because you exude Christ-driven kindness. You will be fulfilled not because of the geographical location but because you practice generosity. You will be free not because your surroundings changed but because you did.

 # Buster

My wife and I recently sat down with my paternal grandmother, NeeNee, to learn about my family tree. Like the cultures that surrounded the events of Scripture, black people have always practiced an oral tradition of passing down history. My family doesn't have books full of our history citing where we originated. The ravaging nature of slavery, for a time, robbed us of such a thing. This only magnified the importance of us spending time with the elders of my family. That being said, sitting with my grandmother and asking her questions about our history was such a rich experience. I didn't just learn names of relatives long gone, having succumbed to the inevitable exit we all will make from the world. No, I learned the character traits that these people embodied as they lived in this world. Many of these traits are still evident in myself and my family members now.

Perhaps the most interesting thing I learned was that my great-great-grandfather, Buster Dillahunty, was a slave. For me, it was one thing to know that, as a black man, my ancestors were enslaved. This I understood. But it was completely different for me to put a name to it and realize that I am a direct descendant of a slave only four generations back. I felt that. But what I primarily felt was not anger, disgust, or grief, though all of those emotions made guest appearances in my soul. Rather, the emotion that took permanent residence in me was pride. My grandmother explained that post-slavery, my family valued education, land ownership, hard work, and faith. My great-grandmother made education non-negotiable. My great-grandfather made land ownership a mandate. They both made hard work and faith the foundation of it all. These characteristics were instilled in my grandmother. As a black woman, she would later raise four boys by herself while completing a college degree at the University of Kansas. She also served as an educator for 50 years. She would pass these traits on to my dad, who would pass them on to me.

The strides of success and achievement in my family history presently end with me, but it all started with Buster. Based upon the oral tradition and the obvious character traits that my family embodies, Buster decided once he was freed that he would let go of slavery. He wasn't going to let the circumstances he was born into define the man he would become. I don't think this was something Buster just knew. I believe he walked this path by the guidance of the Holy Spirit. He knew that his character was more important than his circumstances.

So, allow me to encourage you to change your perspective and prayers. Instead of looking for a new city, ask God to change your character. Instead of fleeing to a place that you perceive has more opportunities, stand firm in the area where God has you. Today, the previously unnoteworthy city of Nazareth is the commonly known birthplace of the Savior. Who knows, maybe the place you're in now will be known for the work you'll do there.

CHAPTER 6
The Security Trap ←

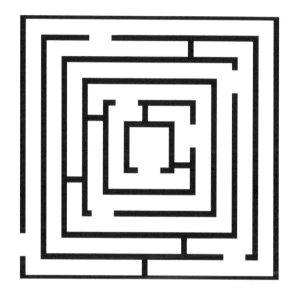

"They left everything and followed Jesus."

Luke 5:11 NLT

Just in Case

My college experience at Hampton University, a historically black college in Hampton, Virginia, was nothing short of amazing. I graduated with a Bachelor of Arts in journalism and a minor in leadership. In school, I forged life-long friendships, met my wife, received a top-grade education, and made memories that will stick with me until my life is over. But if I'm honest, there is still a part of my brain that often thinks it wasn't necessary for me to go to college.

Long before it was time for me to attend HU, I knew God's purpose for my life. It was clear to me. I had no reservations or questions about my calling. So why did I go to a traditional school instead of going straight to Bible college? Truthfully, it was because of my dad. While the decision was ultimately mine, I'd be lying if I said I didn't heavily weigh my father's approval. That's not to say my dad was unsupportive of my dreams. My father believed in me and my calling. However, he was still adamant for me to get a degree in something corporately applicable as a backup plan. I thought, *"What if God doesn't come through?"* It was an insurance policy for my purpose, so to speak.

Just in case it didn't work out, I would have something to fall back on. So, I went to Hampton. It all worked out for me. I met my wife and even started the campus ministry for our school. This was a reminder that God will do his work in me and through me wherever I am. Nevertheless, clearly fear, not faith, drove me to attend HU. It was about having a backup plan just in case God didn't deliver on his promises for my life's purpose. But now, I know God's promises don't need an insurance policy. If God promised it and purposed me to do it, then I don't need insurance because I have his assurance. God's promises will come to fruition.

 ## Insurance Policies

Insurance is a funny thing when you think about it. You pay a company to protect your assets just in case something happens, and if it never happens, you're not reimbursed. Nevertheless, we are all happy, and even in some cases required, to have it. Why? Because it offers a sense of security that you and your assets will be protected. I'm not against insurance. I have insurance for everything I own, including my life. While I believe it's a sign of wisdom to insure your property, I also think it shows a lack of faith when we try to insure our purpose before we step out on faith. Yet this is what so many of us do when we fall into the trap of security. We try to take out an insurance policy before we act in obedience and pursue the purposes of God.

I witnessed the fallacy of security up close in my dad's life. My dad has been in ministry for over 30 years. But for most of that time, he was bi-vocational. He pastored while concurrently working for an organization that insures the state of Arkansas. It was always my dad's heart to work in ministry full-time. Nevertheless, his other job offered him security and financial stability that was not guaranteed in ministry, or so he thought. So, he continued to do ministry and work a full-time corporate job. In 2014, he became the new pastor of a church. It was a smaller church with about 200 people on the roster. The church was financially strong enough to pay him a salary, but his salary was nowhere near the amount that he earned at his regular 9-to-5 job. But that was fine with him. He was close to getting lifetime benefits from his day job, so he planned to work there for a few more years before retiring. Afterwards, he would practice ministry full-time. But then, the unexpected happened.

The day after he started working as the church's new pastor, the bosses at his other job called him into their office. Out of nowhere, they fired him. For 20 years, he served as a stellar leader. He received numerous promotions and celebrated countless achievements. Maybe it would've been better if there were company-wide layoffs. But no, it was just him. After a long and outstanding tenure with the company they just let him go. It seemed cruel. He was so close to retirement.

When I asked my dad how he felt, he said he was at peace. It shocked me at first, but it became clear why my dad felt at peace even though the insurance policy on his purpose had just been cancelled. There is more peace in trusting God's plans completely than there could ever be in trusting in your own. When you trust in God's promises, plans, and purposes, you will never need a backup plan. I think this is what God was teaching my dad. Pushed into his purpose, now he would have to trust in the assurances of God more than the insurance of his day job. He could no longer rely on the security and stability of his day job. My dad would now have to rely totally on the sovereignty of God. Total reliance on him is what God wants from us all.

> *When you trust in God's promises, plans, and purposes, you will never need a backup plan.*

 ## Providers

To be clear, I don't fault my dad for having a plan before betting it all on ministry or his concern about my choice to do so. At the core of most men is an innate desire to provide for themselves and their families. Actually, it is more than a desire. For many, it is the driving force of their lives. For those who walk in faith, it is understood as a God-given responsibility and an act of obedience. I understand my dad's strong desire to make sure that we both did something that provided sufficiently for our families. Historically, vocational ministry didn't guarantee that for many.

Most men understand that it's their duty to make sure their family has the basic necessities of life such as food, water, and shelter. This is what gets some men out of bed each morning. While this responsibility is essential, it can also blind us to one of our other duties: the duty of modeling active faith for our families. Now, I don't mean to exclude women in my remarks. These truths apply to women as well. However, I do believe I've seen more men crippled by this next trap than anyone else because of the natural, God-given duty for men to be providers and protectors. If taken too far, this biblical truth can dampen a man or woman's faith sensors. This may cause them to worry more about being stable and secure and less about exercising faith and taking steps to pursue their destiny.

The *security trap* is the trap of familiarity tied to feeling secure occupationally and financially. People who struggle with the security trap have a secure job that offers steady compensation. The employees see no sense in jeopardizing that security. This sounds like common sense, but sometimes common sense can hinder spiritual advancement. It can cause workers to trust more in their employer than the omnipotent one. The seemingly conventional wisdom of maintaining stability serves as a mind-soothing yet soul-stumbling excuse for disobedience. For many, failure to step out on faith due to concern over occupational or financial security isn't about being responsible. It's about not wanting to take a God-ordained risk. But, they can never experience God's best as long as they play it safe. I'm convinced now more than ever that hearing God say, "Well done!" depends on how often we ask, "Why not?" when faced with God-ordained risks.

 ## Why Not?

I have experienced several "why not" moments in my life. Moments where the Holy Spirit emboldened me to take a leap of faith. Each leap was hard. Come to think of it, they keep getting progressively harder, but God keeps showing me that taking a risk for him isn't really a risk at all.

The most significant "why not" moment in my life was when God revealed that he wanted me and my wife to plant a church. Please understand that church planting was not on my radar. I knew I felt a call to pastor. Nonetheless, because of my frame of reference, I figured I'd just apply for a vacant position at an established church. Or, I could serve in a lower capacity until I was promoted after the senior pastor retired. I never seriously contemplated starting a church. Who in their right mind would? You're starting from scratch most of the time with no money, no building, and no congregation. You at least need that last ingredient to be a church by the New Testament's standards.

With that in mind, starting a church wasn't a dream of mine. However, everything changed when a friend of mine had introduced me to Smokie Norful, a Grammy award-winning Gospel artist and the pastor of Victory Cathedral Worship Center in Bolingbrook, Illinois. Smokie invited me to a mini-conference he was planning in Chicago to help young pastors plant or revitalize churches. I had never been, so I thought, "Why not?" I'd go for the experience if nothing else. I get there, and he begins to roll out his dream. As I listened, all of the challenges of planting a church were present in my subconscious. Then, as Smokie concluded his presentation, seemingly out of nowhere, the Holy Spirit overrides my subconscious and plants a seed. Two words ring in my mind, heart, and soul…*"Why Not?"* It was, at first, a question from God to me, but after praying and fasting, it became a statement from me to God. That day, his Spirit asked my soul, *"Why not trust me? Why not take a chance for me? Why not deviate from the plans for yourself and pursue my purpose?"* Days later, my soul responded, "Why Not! You've never failed me. You have always provided for me. You know more than me. Why not take a risk?"

That was almost six years ago. Since then, I left the staff of two established churches, where I had financial security and stability. My wife and I moved to Minneapolis, Minnesota, a place I never thought I'd live, to launch a new church. We have a dedicated team of believers committed to establishing a healthy church. God has already started using us to help change lives in this city. I don't wish it, but if God hit the stop button on my life right now and brought me home to him, I'm confident he'd say, "Well done" primarily because of my faith in the righteousness of Jesus but also because I gave him my "why not."

Oh, and all of those valid reasons why I didn't want to plant? God took care of that, too. I had no secure income when we moved. Four years later, my family's needs have always been met. My wife and I have never been late on a bill. We've never missed a meal, yet we had no congregation. In less than a year, God sent thirty people, and now, we have even more. We had no space, so we moved into a 200-seat sanctuary.

> **God's affirming "well done" is preceded by our faith-filled "why not."**

I firmly believe that God's affirming "well done" is preceded by our faith-filled "why not." In the middle of your "why not" and God's "well done" is his comforting assurance: "I'm With You."

A Deal with God on a Snowy Day

Mark Batterson is one of my favorite authors. I recommend for you to read everything he's ever written. I guarantee you'll come away feeling like you've wrestled a lion. In fact, one of his most popular books is called *In a Pit with a Lion on a Snowy Day*. God linked my life to Mark, though I've never met him. I don't know how to explain it. He always releases a book at just the right moment in my life. I don't think it's a coincidence that the day God called me to have immense faith in his promises, it was a snowy day in Arkansas, and I felt like I was facing a lion.

God's Word and his promises undergird my confidence when giving him my "why not." Jesus told us not to worry. He promised that he'd provide for us (Matthew 6:25–33; Philippians 4:19). However, years later, I can tell you it's not just his Word that gives me confidence, but my personal walk with him. I used to believe based on what the Word explained. Now, I believe because of what I've experienced.

I like to tell people that God and I made a deal when I accepted my call to preach. In truth, his assurance calmed my soul from the anxiety of the assignment he placed on my life. I'll never forget that day. I was a 14-year-old freshman in high school, and it was snowing, which was a rarity in Arkansas. I laid on my bed, wrestling with God about the weight of the calling I felt in my life. We had been in a wrestling match for a while now. I knew he wanted me to preach, but I had plans of my own. I didn't want to preach or do ministry. I was young, and I wanted to be normal. I still had so many inconsistencies and cracks in my character. Plus, my dad was in ministry, and he had always told me how fickle it can be. *Surely you don't want that for me, God.* Every excuse I could think of, I hurled at God.

But eventually, I grew weary of trying to subdue the sovereign, so I finally submitted to his plans for my life. Pinned by the purpose of God, I asked for his assurance. My promise went like this, *"God, if you will provide for me and my family through the work of ministry, I'll go wherever you want me to go and do whatever you want me to do."* With all my heart, I believe that day he said, "I'm with you." That occurred nearly fourteen years ago. It has been an incredible journey, but the most amazing thing is that God has kept and continues to keep his promise. In fourteen years,

I have never done any work outside of vocational ministry. I've lived in four states and served at four churches. I've taken pay cuts numerous times, but I have always had enough for my wife and me. Not only have we always had enough, but there have also been a few times when we've had more than enough.

That day I traded in my plans for God's purpose and received his promise: "I'm with you." I continue to ask God "why not" because he has never failed on that promise. It isn't just something I know cognitively. It's something I've known experientially. When you pursue God's purpose, he will take care of your provision. If you step out on faith, he will handle your finances. I know the job may be familiar, the pay makes you feel safe, but if you're sure God has called you to do something, then be wise. Plan, but most importantly, trade your security in the world for the surety of God's promises. It will lead to a purposeful life.

Leaving Everything Behind

"They left everything and followed Jesus." Luke 5:11 NLT

At times we forget that the biblical figures depicted in Scripture were real people, not merely characters of some fictional story. They were individuals whose actions and faith had real consequences. When we remember that reality, it brings so much more weight to what we read in Scripture.

That reality hit me as I read the last line of Luke 5:11. The preceding verses chronicle how the apostle Simon Peter came to be a follower of the Lord, Jesus Christ. One day, Jesus borrowed a boat from Peter, sat down, and began teaching people from it. Following his teaching, he gives Peter, who just experienced a failed night of fishing, some divine tips. As a result, Peter catches more fish than he can handle. Subsequently, Jesus told him that his job catching fish foreshadowed the purpose God had for him. It wasn't to catch fish but to help catch souls for Christ. In the shadow of this encounter, "they left everything and followed Jesus." This, I believe, is one of the most radical lines in Scripture.

That day Peter laid down his fishing gear and became a full-time follower of Jesus and pursuer of his purpose. Now, let me explain something to you. Peter is not laying down a hobby. Peter is laying down his livelihood. He was a professional fisherman. That's how he provided security and stability for his family and for himself. But Peter wasn't going to get caught in the trap of familiar security. He decided he would trust in the security offered only by making faith moves. We should be glad about that! If Peter had been more concerned about where his provisions were coming from than he did about pursuing God's purpose, he would have missed what God wanted to do in him. The world would have missed out on what God wanted to do through him. Peter never would have preached and seen 3,000 people saved in one day. He wouldn't have helped establish the Church. He never would have written two books in the New Testament, and we never would have known that Jesus can forgive us, even when we act like we don't know him.

Peter set an example for you and me. Don't let the trap of security stop you from allowing God to use you. Don't let fear keep you from what God wants to do in you. You can't afford to miss it, and neither can the world. So, leave everything behind and pursue God. Pursue his purpose for you!

CHAPTER 7
The Success Trap ←

"Not that I have already reached the goal or am already perfect,
but I make every effort to take hold of it because
I also have been taken hold of by Christ Jesus.
Brothers and sisters, I do not consider myself to have taken
hold of it. But one thing I do: Forgetting what is behind
and reaching forward to what is ahead."

Philippians 3:12–14 CSB

Coming to Arkansas

My wife likes to jokingly tell others I am the Arkansas version of Prince Akeem from the popular 80's movie *Coming to America,* starring Eddie Murphy. It's her way of saying that in Arkansas, I'm like royalty. This is absolutely an exaggeration. I promise! The truth is, Little Rock is a small city. My parents are very social, so I had the honor of getting to know many people, some of whom were considered important figures in the community. That being said, I benefited tremendously from relationships there, and I was afforded opportunities to be a part of some very special moments. Frankly put, God allowed me to experience favor and success in the city where I grew up. Ironically, this is exactly why I believe God didn't want me to stay there for that season. Staying would have surely landed me in what I call the success trap, ultimately keeping me from God's best for my life.

The ***success trap*** occurs when you've been successful somewhere, and you stay because it's familiar. People know you and may even admire you. You've accomplished a lot. However, this trap keeps you from God's best. Successful people tend to rely on their own reputation instead of God's power. Relying on yourself and your own accomplishments is not only a recipe for a prideful heart, but it's also the surest way to miss the fullness of God's purpose for your life. Once you embrace God's plan for your life, the most important thing to remember is that you will only be able to accomplish it with his help. The success trap often blinds us to this truth, and it keeps us from going after big dreams.

 ## Big Fish Need Bigger Ponds

You've probably heard the phrase "big fish in a little pond." It's an anecdote for someone who thrives where it's easy for them. It's also a reflection of someone who is seen as a big deal, but only in comparison to people who are perceived as less accomplished. Maybe you're the big fish I'm speaking of. If you're going to reach your fullest potential, it's imperative for you to learn about the deceptive nature of the success trap.

The success trap wants to keep the big fish (that's you) in the little pond by appealing to the fish's pride. The enemy will stoke a fire in your soul, convincing you that you have "arrived." He'll make you think that you've accomplished everything, you've ascended to the best social status, and you're a success. He doesn't want you to realize that there are bigger ponds where God wants to take you.

I don't think being a big fish in a little pond is about you being better than the pond. It's really about you growing as much as you can within that pond. It is less of an indictment on what the pond has to offer and more of an indication that you have given and received as much as you could from it. When you look at it from this perspective, the truth becomes clear. For the people submitted to God's plans and purposes, there comes a season in all of your lives when you become big fish in little ponds. Eventually, you will hit the ceiling for what God wanted to accomplish through you in that place.

When it happens, it's important to remember that your success doesn't mean you've "arrived" in life. Instead, you should adopt the apostle Paul's attitude. He knew that he hadn't achieved perfection in Christ, and he didn't put too much stock on his achievements. Rather than dwell on his past accomplishments, he strengthened his relationship with God while pursuing his God-given purpose (Philippians 3:12–14). Even though Paul had grown as big as he could in some ponds, he knew God wanted to take him to bigger ponds. God wanted to mold Paul's character to be more Christ-like. God wanted to use Paul to make a difference in the world. To do this, Paul couldn't sit on his successes. He needed to make faith moves and travel to bigger ponds.

The same is true for you. God wants to take you to bigger ponds because he knows it's the only way you'll become a bigger fish. Trust God in new spaces, new jobs, new church communities, new areas of service, and perhaps even new cities where you have not had previous success. This is the only way to reach your fullest potential in Christ and see the fullness of God's power. If you never go to a place that requires more of you, how will you know how much God has placed inside of you? If you never go to a place that requires more faith, how will you know how much trust you have in God? If you never go to a place that requires a miracle from God, how will you know that he's able? Bigger ponds bring out greater purpose. God wants to show you something new about his power. He wants you to see the depth of your purpose, but before you can leave your small pond, you will first need faith.

 ## New Level

    I still remember the thought that ran through my mind when I moved to Hampton, Chicago, and Minneapolis. This isn't going to sound spiritual because it's not. I wrestled with the reality that I was going to have re-establish my reputation as an influential preacher. I'd have to start over and prove myself again. That thought tried to bother me. Forgive me if this sounds carnal, but I'm just being honest. Thank God the Holy Spirit intervened! He quickly reminded me that I didn't preach for my reputation. I preach for the glory of the Father. God also soothed my carnal concerns by reminding me that it's not about starting over. It's about starting at a new level. That's the same encouragement I want to give you. If you're like me, you might hesitate to leave your current pond because you don't want to start over in a new space. It seems much more appealing to bask in past success than to pursue something new.

    Life is far from a game, but for just a moment, imagine that it is. As an avid video game player when I was younger (I still dabble in them now), one of my favorite games was called "Kingdom Hearts." I'll spare you the details, but it was a quest game. Unlike sports games or combat games, the objective of a quest game is to pursue new levels while mastering skills before facing the big boss in the final level. Some levels took me forever to beat. I seriously would devote all of my time and intellect to beat them. As trivial as it may seem now, few feelings rivaled the level of accomplishment I felt when I completed those levels. However, winning one level was not the end goal. The reason I played was to face the big boss in the final level.

I live life while pursuing my God-given purpose for the same reason: to see the big boss at the end. Not to challenge him but to be commended by him to hear "well done." I know I'll hear "well done" because I've trusted in Jesus as my Savior. I'd also love to hear "well done" because I beat the levels of life where he called me to place more of my faith in him. With that being said, if I spend too much time focusing on the last level of accomplishment, I'll miss what God has in store for me right now. So, don't think of stepping into something new as starting over. Think of it as starting a new level. Celebrate the level you beat while also remembering that you're working to be commended by the big boss at the last level.

Success is often the enemy of progress. Leaving memories of success in the past helps us remain dependent on God in the present while remaining humble. More than anything, God wants us to trust him and to lean on him. This is where most of us have a hard time. We have trouble deciding which to trust: God's plans or our plans. But we must pick one. His name or our own name. His reputation or our own reputation. We cannot completely trust God while completely trusting ourselves.

As you ponder on who you will trust, allow me to share truths from my own life. Every time I trusted my own intellect, gifts, or reputation, I fell on my face. But every time I trusted God, things turned out better than I could have ever imagined. For me, it's a no-brainer. If you want to reach your potential, then I encourage you to choose the same. Pick God over yourself. Get over yourself and your past successes. Trust God. He has more in store for you than you could ever imagine!

CHAPTER 8
The Self Trap ⟵

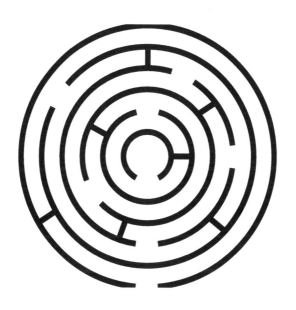

"For whoever wants to save his life
will lose it, but whoever loses his life
because of me will find it."

Matthew 16:25 CSB

This last trap is tricky. It's the **self trap.**

The spring for it is triggered not by external circumstances but rather by our own internal consciousness. Most humans go through years, even decades, of insecurity about who they are. The discovery of one's personality, likes and dislikes, beliefs, and convictions is a journey. What keeps us from reaching our fullest potential is believing that the journey ends. I think this happens more than we realize. We become familiar with ourselves, who we are, and what we think we know. We leave no room for God to teach us more. It's a self trap. Reaching your God-given potential depends on how well you know yourself. However, you cannot be stubbornly familiar with yourself.

 ## Be Settled, Not Stubborn

Now, I want to be sure to put some parameters around this. We should be settled in our beliefs and our core convictions. We must know who God is and how we can get to know him. We must know the truth of who we are made to be. However, we must leave room for what we don't know about ourselves and the depths of the gifts that God has placed inside of us. It's a delicate dance.

I told you about my friend Peter Williams who often says, "Be humble to take advice, but trust the Spirit in you enough to make your own decision." The same principle applies to the self trap. We should live our lives with humility, knowing that God teaches us more about himself and ourselves every day. Simultaneously, we should be confident in what he's already shown us. We should be settled but not stubborn. We may know what God has called us to do today, but we have no idea what he might lead us to do tomorrow. We may know the dreams he's given us today, but who knows what dreams he'll reveal tomorrow? Don't limit what God may desire of you by thinking that he'd never want to use you in new ways.

Losing Myself

I mentioned earlier that church planting was never something I thought I'd do. In fact, I'll embarrassingly admit that in the arrogance of my youth, I used to criticize people who started or planted churches. Due to my limited frame of reference, my uninformed opinion was God didn't need more churches. He just needed better ones. God sure has a sense of humor. Years later, I'm a church planter! The funny thing is that

I never imagined it because I thought I was familiar with myself. I felt sure about the trajectory of my ministry. But boy, was I wrong! Realizing I was wrong, at times, made me feel like I was losing myself. At first, that scared me. Then God reminded me that losing yourself is the surest way to find your purpose.

> **Losing yourself is the surest way to find your purpose.**

The Bible reveals to us that the kingdom of God is full of paradoxes. If you want to be exalted, you have to be humble. If you want to receive more, you should give more. And if you want to save your life, you have to be willing to lose it. It's the same principle for discovering your purpose. If you want to find yourself, you have to lose yourself. Now is the perfect time for you to listen to Eminem's song (another dad joke). Before becoming who God wants you to be, you must first let go of who you think you should be. If you're afraid to lose the person you are, you'll never discover the person God destined you to be.

 ## The Right View

I was right about what God called me to do, which was the first step. But I still needed to remain humble enough to receive God's teaching about how he wanted me to do it. That meant allowing God to replace my thoughts with his thoughts of me every single day. It meant losing myself.

Everyone has a view of who they are now in their head. Simultaneously, most people envision who they want to be in the future. The issue is most of us have factored some of our current characteristics into our future selves. We imagine that in the future, we'll be in better circumstances. But if we're honest, most of us haven't dreamt about our different, more Christ-like character. We know we want the things around us to change, but we don't think much about how we should change. God is more interested in changing our character than he is our circumstances. So reaching your God-given potential isn't primarily about getting to a place; it's about becoming a new person. You

> *You can't reach your full potential and still remain the same person you are today.*

can't reach your full potential and still remain the same person you are today. But, that's ok. I fight to trust who God is changing me to be every day. The one thing I can say is, so far, his view has been so much better than mine. I guarantee that the person he's trying to mold you into will be better than who you are right now.

CHAPTER 9
Faith Moves ←

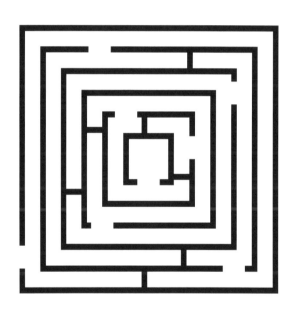

As a young preacher, I was taught that a sermon isn't really a sermon if you don't have a call to action for the listeners. I listed several throughout this book. Here is a recap just in case you didn't write them down.

1. ***Be bold and step into unfamiliar surroundings.***
2. ***Don't cling to what you know.***
3. ***Stop avoiding what you don't know.***
4. ***Have faith in God and pursue your God-given purpose.***

 ## The Order of Love

While I was a preteen, I attended a Christian summer camp called Kids Across America. While attending this camp, I gave my life to Jesus. In addition to understanding my sin and the need for Jesus to save me, I learned something very important here. They taught us the order of who should receive our love and attention. It's simple yet so profound: love God first, my neighbor second, and myself last. Adopted correctly, following this order should help govern our decisions to reflect Christ. But as I thought about this order, I realized it's not just a wonderful guide for how to love. It was also a guide for how to move past our familiar surroundings. If you're going to get out of the traps, you'll need faith in God, support from others, and belief in yourself.

Faith in God

Without faith, it is impossible to please God. Therefore, without faith it is impossible to reach your fullest potential in God. I once heard Andy Stanley, the pastor of North Point Community Church, define faith in a sermon series called "Welcome to Wonderland." He said, "Faith is the confidence that God is and will do what he promised to do. And we believe God will keep his promises because God has kept his promises." He crystallizes faith by reminding us that faith isn't blind hope. Rather, it is trust in the one who has proven himself to be trustworthy. If we're going to move away from the familiar while avoiding pitfalls, we must trust in the God who has shown himself to be trustworthy in the past.

The Bible is the ultimate historical record of God's faithfulness. He proves over and over again that he is our provider, our protector, our guide, and everything else we need. But maybe you don't need to focus on just biblical history. Consider your personal history as well. I'm confident that there have been moments in your life where you took a leap. It may have been a small one or a big one. But you leaped, and God caught you. He showed himself trustworthy. To quote gospel artist Tye Tribbett, "If he did it before, he can do it again."

You have to trust God. You have to move by faith. There's no getting around it. Without faith, it's impossible to please God. Without faith, it's impossible to reach your fullest potential in God.

Support from Others

Humans weren't made to go through life alone. Relationships are everything; they're essential to our earthly experience. We have to be careful not to allow our relationships to hold us back. But, also we can't forget that God often uses people as his instrument for pushing us forward.

I can trace almost every dream God has given me back to a person he placed in my life. Most of those people not only inspired the dream, but they also encouraged me as I pursued it. Sometimes that encouragement was loving. Sometimes it was challenging. It's the challenging kind of encouragement that often gets us out of the traps of familiarity. The kind that says, "Be bold! Be brave! Break free!"

Even though we weren't really friends at the time, I have a friend named Marc who challenged me. It was right around the time I was hearing from God about planting a church. We were having a conversation about ministry and my next steps. I was unsure whether this was what God wanted for me to pursue. All of a sudden, Marc said, "Man, I don't want to hear that crap! You know exactly what God is calling you to do. You're just acting like a punk." My mouth dropped. In my head, I was calling him something other than a child of God. Who was this guy to tell me I was acting scared? Finally, I stopped thinking about it and let the Holy Spirit speak. Then, I realized Marc was right. I knew what needed to be done, but the courage in me was waning. I needed to be challenged by someone who wasn't going to accept my excuses. We all do. The truth is God has given you everything you need to move from what's familiar. He uses people to remind you he's given you everything you need. If you're going to get out, you'll need to lean on and accept support from others—both the loving kind and the challenging kind.

Believe in Yourself

Let me be clear about what I mean when I say believe in yourself: I mean to believe in who God says you are and what God says you can do. It has often been said that the Bible is God's love letter to us. I believe that's true. In that love letter, he tells us over and over again who we are. He tells us we're more than conquerors. He tells us that we are free in Christ Jesus. He tells us that we are loved. He even tells us that the same spirit that raised Jesus from the grave is inside us (Romans 8:11). God doesn't just tell us that we are loved. He tells us who we are because of that love. You're adopted into his divine family. You're chosen by him to bear his name and do miraculous things on the earth on his behalf. You are not an ordinary person. You are not someone destined to be born, pay bills, and die. He has made you with a purpose. Escape what's familiar by remembering that you were made for so much more. Believe that. Believe in yourself.

CHAPTER *10*
Life Outside the Trap ←

You know, a lot of people believe that being a Christian is no fun. Secretly, there are probably some practicing Christians who believe it, but that's because they're not doing it right. They have relegated Christianity to a set of "don't" rules, but that's not what following Jesus is about. Being a true follower of Jesus is about what you're willing to do for God, just as much as it is about what you're not supposed to do. I'd even say it's more about stepping out on faith to do great things for God because of grace than to avoid sinning because you're afraid of God. When you understand that, you realize that following Jesus is pretty fun.

A life of faith is a life of fun. It's not the "sit by the beach and sip on a coconut" kind of fun. It's the "go to Six Flags and ride all of the rides" kind of fun. Or, the "hike up a mountain" kind of fun. It's an adventure, and God is your tour guide. You're constantly pursuing new paths while simultaneously discovering the depth of your own potential. You're dreaming new dreams and taking unknown risks. You're putting yourself out there and letting God constantly reshape who you are. It's a life full of faith moves. That's a pretty exciting life if you ask me. That's the life waiting for you outside of the traps of familiarity. A life of faith is the life that God wants you to live. So, go do it! Make a move! You never know. The move you make today might put you in the middle of a movement tomorrow.

WORKS CITED

"Aaliyah Plane was Overloaded by Hundreds of Pounds." CNN.com, 31 Aug. 2001. https://edition.cnn.com/2001/WORLD/americas/08/30/aaliyah. crash/.

Batterson, Mark. In a Pit with a Loin on a Snowy Day: How to Survive and Thrive When Opportunity Roars. The Crown Publishing Group, 2016.

Cloud, Henry. The Power of the Other: The Startling Effect Other People Have on You, from the Boardroom to the Bedroom and Beyond—and What to do About It. HarperCollins Publishers, 2016.

Columbus, Chris, director. Home Alone 2: Lost in New York. Twentieth Century Fox, 1992.

Coraci, Frank, director. The Waterboy. Touchstone Pictures, 1998.

DeYoung, Kevin. Just Do Something: A Liberating Approach to Finding God's Will. Moody Publishers, 2014.

DJ Jazzy Jeff & the Fresh Prince. "Parents Just Don't Understand." He's the DJ, I'm the Rapper. Calhoun Productions, 1988.

McLeod, Saul. "Maslow's Hierarchy of Needs." Simply Psychology. 29 Dec. 2020. www.simplypsychology.org/maslow.html.

Meyers, Nancy, director. The Parent Trap. Walt Disney Pictures, 1998.

"NTSB Identification: MIA01RA225." National Transportation Safety Board. https://www.ntsb.gov/_layouts/15/ntsb.aviation/brief2.aspx?ev_ id=20010907X01905&ntsbno=MIA01RA225&akey=1.

Spielberg, Steven, director. Indiana Jones and the Last Crusade. Paramount Pictures, 1989.

Made in the USA
Columbia, SC
31 July 2022

64259905R00057